TINY GIANT:

CONQUER YOUR FEARS
WITH CHIHUAHUA
COURAGE

Written by Edouard Atangana

ACKNOWLEDGMENT

As we release this book into the world—a meditation on the timeless battle with our innermost fears—it feels both humbling and deeply moving to reflect on the journey that brought us here. Today, on Good Friday, a cornerstone of the Christian tradition, we are reminded of the ultimate narrative of courage and sacrifice that has resonated through the ages: the story of Jesus Christ. His life, unjustly ended on the cross, was a testament to facing and overcoming fear in all its forms. From the fear of standing alone against a prevailing and unjust system to the intimate fears of rejection, misunderstanding, and failure, Jesus's journey encapsulates the essence of our own struggles with fear.

In penning this book, my heart is filled with gratitude for the myriad souls who have walked with me on this path. To those who have stood by me, offering their encouragement and strength, allowing me to face the cacophony of fears within, I owe a debt that words can scarcely capture. The 'Chihuahua within'—our metaphor for the fears that bark loudly but have little real power to harm us—represents the universal battle each of us faces. We all harbor fears, big and small, that challenge us to grow, adapt, and ultimately, to find peace and purpose amidst life's tumult.

This acknowledgment extends beyond a simple thank you; it is a celebration of our shared human experience. To my friends, advisors, family members, and to everyone who has ever felt the grip of fear, your resilience is a beacon. Your struggles and triumphs have not only inspired this work but have also shown that fear, no matter how daunting, can be confronted and conquered.

Let the story of Jesus, beyond its religious and spiritual dimensions, serve as a powerful reminder of what it means to truly conquer fear. His life was not just about facing fears; it was about transcending them to fulfill a mission of love, compassion, and transformation. In his example, we find a profound lesson in how to live our own lives with courage and purpose.

To all who have ever felt fear yet pressed on, who have faced the unknown and walked forward regardless, this book is for you. Thank you for not giving up, for in your perseverance, you embody the very essence of courage. Together, let us continue on our journey towards a more meaningful, fear-conquered life inspired by the greatest story of resilience known to humanity.

McAllen, Texas

March 29, 2024

Dedication

To Dr. Eugenio G. Galindo, MD,

In the intricate mosaic of existence, where grandiosity often eclipses the seemingly insignificant, the true measure of valor is found in the essence of courage. 'Tiny Giants: Conquering Our Fears with a Chihuahua Courage' is dedicated to you, Dr. Galindo, as an emblem of the steadfast bravery and resilience that you both embody and awaken within others.

Mirroring the indomitable spirit of the Chihuahua—petite in form yet boundless in heart— you have showcased that genuine courage emanates not from physical might, but from the profound depths of the soul and the unwavering resolve to effect change. Your devotion to healing, your empathy for those in your care, and your relentless commitment to the vanguard of medicine encapsulate the very courage this book seeks to celebrate.

Let this dedication stand as a mirror to our immense gratitude and respect for your indefatigable spirit and infinite courage. You illuminate the truth that giants manifest in myriad forms, proving that it is the magnitude of one's determination, rather than their stature, that truly delineates their grandeur.

With utmost admiration and heartfelt thanks,

Fr. Edouard Atangana, PhD, STL

TABLE OF CONTENTS

THE BARKING

Again, you wake up feeling tired, bothered by those nights where you feel like you didn't sleep. You perceive it like this: you lay down on the mattress, adjusted your pillow, closed your eyes, and saw darkness. Then you opened your eyes, and only a few seconds had passed, but it was already the next morning!

Did you rest? Of course not.

These nights happen more often than you'd like to admit, and you think something is bothering you, something that lurks in your head and stalks you. They are questions; you know it well. Alone or with a company, you've found yourself turning your neck left and right, staring at a non-existent point; you wonder if what you're doing is what you'd like to be doing. You also reflect on the number of activities you'd like to undertake but haven't.

Have you asked yourself what you'd like to experience that you aren't experiencing? Or simply, how would you like your life to be?

This book is not a magic guide to take you to that place where you think you want to be, and I'd be lying if I said it was. Let's be clear from the start, no one is ever in a completely perfect situation. Even those characters who seem to have everything are not completely satisfied.

Think, for example, of the swimmer Michael Phelps. He won twenty-three Olympic gold medals, set records, and accumulated several million dollars, all before turning forty. Despite his daily physical training and excellent diet, Michael Phelps was not, nor is a healthy individual. He suffers from depression and even had such a negative streak that after the Olympics, he locked himself in his hotel room and didn't come out for days. Phelps has hit rock bottom many times.

Now, let's focus on the opposite case and think about artists who dedicated themselves completely to their art and the creation of their pieces. There are many examples of painters who did not earn enough money to eat from Monday to Friday but who were happy beings for the possibility of investing their time in what they were most passionate about.

They did not have the security that money and Phelps' fame provide, but they possessed the emotional stability that the excellent swimmer so lacks.

What I am trying to say with these examples is that the concrete formula we have been told about the meaning or the path to happiness (professional success and monetary wealth) is closer to being the direct path to paralyzing fear.

When I say that there is no ideal place where we would like to be, I am referring to the ideal place that we have been made to believe exists. Why do I assert that there is no such place? Because humans always are afraid, and in the definition of the "ideal place," there is no fear.

We all are afraid, Phelps, the artists, you, and I. It is our common point because fear is human.

We can count on our family, live in the house of our dreams, work combining our vocation and professional success, and take trips we have always longed for, or we can have all this and still harbor fear that things will change.

Life's only constant is change. One day may lift us high, while the next may bring us low. The absence of absolute certainty can be daunting. The knowledge that circumstances are prone to flux instills a sense of fear: the possibility of sudden job loss, a flaw surfacing in our home, or the departure of a loved one from our side. Life is a long succession of decision-making and changes at every moment; it is uncontrollable, and the lack of control scares us.

So, if we all are afraid, does that mean that ideal place can exist, right? Of course, with the condition that fear is always present.

My opinion is no. Why is there no ideal place? Why do I dare to say that even with fear, no one fully reaches that ideal place?

Because human life is a work in progress, and we are unfinished beings. We build very high walls only to tear them down later and start over. That's how we are, changing and relentless, fleeting and latent. No one concludes their process during life because, until the day we depart, we will be learning and projecting a colossal transformation.

Life is tension and movement, and the questions that concern us today are the ones that will shape us tomorrow. All the questions that arise throughout our construction have answers, even though the windows, doors, and corridors may seem unfinished. Don't get tired of answering your own questions, and always dare to let curiosity be one of the most valuable ingredients of your building.

Sometimes, our project in the process reveals the guidelines and frameworks that are followed to build. In a way, we can observe inside the models and plans based on which we have built ourselves. We can delve into our past and look at the connection of nodes that led us here.

On the other hand, sometimes, the project cracks a little and shows us the fears and obstacles that prevent us from continuing the work. We come across land that needs to be sifted, with a lack of equipment and workforce, with the need for permits and licenses. When the project stops, it is because fear has invaded it. If you feel that your life has become perennial, it is because you are not answering your own questions, and it is because you are not generating more doubts because fear has complete control.

The fears that prevent us from living what we really want, leading the life we want, or continuing to forge ourselves as what we want to be are the most dangerous fears. These fears do not make noise nor produce initial symptoms.

It is precisely these silent fears that manipulate us the most. If you stop asking yourself how to proceed with your project, it is because your fear forbids you from asking the right questions, and you have become a hostage to your fear, locking yourself in your comfort zone.

In any case, there is always a breaking point, a crucial moment that will force you to make a decision. Feeling that you are not resting or lacking concentration for your daily tasks are two examples of an impending earthquake. You yourself rebel against that fear that keeps you exhausted.

Then, one day, you wake up, stretch, and sigh just like yesterday and the day before, you are very tired and if you look at yourself in the mirror, you might not even recognize yourself. You don't like those pointy ears and stick out your tongue, feeling sick. First, you detect something in the mirror and turn to the floor to check it. You are afraid that your shadow is bigger than you. You notice that you are shaking, that your skin is bristling, and that your teeth are chattering. You are completely sure that you have lost a lot of height. From here, every object looks different and it's not the same perspective.

You look deeply into your small round eyes. You don't recognize yourself. You don't like your dark nose, your prominent snout, or your long claws. You are small, ridiculously small! That displeases you extremely. With fear and disappointment, you exclaim in front of your reflection: "I don't want this!"

And you only hear your barks. Yes, you are a tiny golden chihuahua dog. You feel helpless and disappointed.

You leave the room, and there is that mirror that shows you your condition. You leave carefully, and you don't know what kind of elements you might encounter on the cold floor. Above all, you sense that you have to be careful in the garden. Sometimes, there are sharp objects that someone has forgotten.

When you get to the stairs, you would like to let out a sigh and manage to bark before jumping from one step to another. Each time you hit the ground, you feel your head throb, you remind yourself that you have to be careful going down and you wouldn't want to trip and fall. It would hurt a lot, and you go cautiously. Those steps have felt like a steep hill. Finally, you are on a flat surface again.

You go to the kitchen, but first, you have to pass through the living room. Watch out! Someone threw a cushion. You saw it flying through the air, you saw it approaching you, and you ran fast; it almost hit your face. With your size, you must be careful of many things because you don't want to get hurt. You feel how your heart raced with the change of speed, and you stop a bit to pant and relax. You are frightened.

In the kitchen, you realize that you can hardly reach anything and all the food represents a challenge to your physical ability and your ingenuity. You decide to go out for fresh air and the situation worsens.

On the street, there are huge cars and noisy motorcycles. Each time one passes, you jump. You are nervous; it is better to find another place to be, and you lie down next to a rose bush. The grass is painful; your new figure is uncomfortable. You get up again and approach the concrete that burns.

You are desperate and uncomfortable again with the projection of your shadow on the floor. It is long, longer than you, and it seems that your own silhouette is looking at you with audacity, you pant annoyed because you do not want this dog's life, but this is what you have because this is how you feel like a helpless, frightened, and tiny chihuahua dog.

You bark, jump, dodge, and are on the defensive because you are not able to calm down, even if those around you ask you to. Some justify you by saying that you are nervous, and you know that the reality is that you feel a very deep fear, and that is why you act with so much instability and restlessness.

Neither the hard grass nor the sharp rose bushes are good hiding places. You have to go back to the room where you started and going up the stairs is difficult again, but the hope of finding a place to rest encourages you.

Irremediably, you stand in front of the mirror again and observe your features once more; the dark nose, pointy ears, small pink tongue, and front claws.

You are a trembling Chihuahua dog barking in desperation.

And I ask you: What are you barking at?

We bark when we are lost so we can be found.

We bark when we are confused, so the echo of our voice may bring some answers.

We bark when we are scared to ask for help.

We bark at a situation when we feel alarmed.

Barking is a common, quite primitive action; it's sometimes a beneficial impulse. At my workplace, I encounter people daily who feel like Chihuahua dogs.

-Hello- they greet me timidly as they enter my office.

-Hello- I reply - How can I help you?

-I have a problem-

They begin to tell me personal circumstances that position them in difficult places; spots where light's entry is not accessible, I listen and try to understand. Any of us could reach one of these points unintentionally, as what I hear every day are stories that begin and stall in fear.

Everyone has fears, absolutely everyone, and fear is an inherently human condition. Anyone who says they have no fear is lying, as every action carries its load of fear; from jumping off a cliff to deciding to share the rest of our life with someone.

Fear is a condition for life, and adults teach the young to be cautious and to fear the consequences of thoughtless acts.

Think of a four-year-old child; he likes to run, jump over playground equipment, and swing, and he does not measure risks, just as he does not correctly gauge distances. Children at that age run with their eyes fixed on a point at their height and do not see the ground as they lift one foot and let it fall.

Therefore, there is a high probability that this four-year-old child will fall while heading towards the slide. Imagine it! He runs, dodging a stone here and there, but does not detect a pothole in the path and falls. It's going to hurt.

Then, he will have to check the wound and receive attention; the next time he runs, he will be more careful. The fear of falling again will provoke him, and he will not want the pain or the tears. If he remembers this event, he won't fall as easily next time.

However, he will continue to run. He will also learn that jumping from the swing is dangerous because he might not land on his feet, that throwing himself from the slide without hands implies more risks due to increased speed, and that crossing the monkey bars carries the probability of falling.

Yes, throughout his first years, the child will discover that many situations he enjoys involve a possible accident. He will learn to live with it, and his fear will not paralyze him but make him cautious.

If this child discovers at an early age that he is accompanied by his fear (by his family, friends, and religious belief system), he will become a secure, just, and strong man. He will learn to bring out the best in himself in various situations and become an ally of his fear.

In the Bible, we find several examples of characters who managed to deal with their fear. They achieved this for a simple but powerful reason: God explained to them that they were not alone. The story of David and Goliath is a narrative of trust and security.

How could David, a boy with a sling, defeat someone like Goliath, a nearly three-meter-tall soldier? The story explains that Goliath was a cruel Philistine who used to mock the Israelites. On the other hand, David was an Israeli boy who fully trusted in his god. It was by his faith that he decided to confront Goliath and, chose five smooth stones from a nearby river and went to meet Goliath. When the giant soldier saw him, he thought that ending David's life would be easy. Goliath had a shield and a sword; David had his skill and his sling. Added to this, David harbored complete hope that Jehovah, his god, would use him as an instrument. If he won this encounter, David would save the Israelites from the oppression of the Philistines.

David was brave and set his fear aside, representing his people. A single shot from his sling was enough to hit Goliath right in the head and kill him. David's strongest weapon was his full confidence.

Another example I like to use from the Bible is one of the many stories of Moses. When God asks him to free the Jewish people, Moses is frightened and does not believe himself capable. God is patient with him; he does not demand that he fulfill the request. God waits, and when he tells him again that he will be in charge of taking his people out of Egypt's dominion, Moses doubts because he knows that the pharaoh has a huge army with vehicles, animals, and weapons.

The Jews have absolutely nothing; they are tired and weak.

God is patient and asks Moses again to free his people. Moses justifies himself with the explanation that he is only one man. Then God explains to him that he will be with him all the time and that he will never leave him alone. It is for this reason that Moses overcomes his fear and decides to follow God's instructions and free the Jewish people.

God was patient. He waited for Moses to fully absorb what he wanted to tell him: you are capable even if you don't believe it. God's message is clear; no situation can overwhelm us. Although the length of our shadow may overwhelm us, the sun always positions itself at the highest point and shines. Light unifies us. Fear is with us, but without paralyzing us.

In the New Testament, Saint Paul mentions that one who loves is not afraid. Love is the element that prevents us from feeling fear. This is because love is based on trust and faith.

Throughout the book of Exodus, we learn how God sent his people with a specific mission. That is to say, we are here to fulfill something. God created us with excellent harmony, gifts, and virtues to carry out our tasks. God sent us with love, and that is why we must not allow fear to win. God is on our side.

The previous biblical examples are to understand that fear is natural and human.

New tasks demand that we try harder break our routine; such an event scares us; however, above fear, there is love and trust. These are the key tools to continue through life feeling accompanied and secure.

Within our humanity, we share dreams, spaces, resources, obstacles, and dynamics. Living together with others, the endless friction between us turns fear into a functional feeling. It is important to know that we are never alone, that we do not live on a deserted island, and that we can always get out of the hole where we have gotten ourselves into.

Imagine you are in a beautiful car. It's a '69 Mustang, blue, and the sky partially reflects on the hood. The road runs between ancient mountains, lush trees, and stunning landscapes.

You know the power of the engine and know that you can increase the speed, grab the steering wheel firmly, and have fun driving. You would very much like to do it because, in fact, you are going very slow. But you don't.

You are not running that Mustang the way it was thought, as it was designed and made.

The car is asking you for a gear change, you hear that the engine is being improperly forced, and you just have to move the lever and shift from third to fourth. It's your responsibility, entirely yours, to attend to your fear and overcome it. You are not letting your car function properly; both of you are going to run out of air.

Although we have support networks, people who want to push us and motivate us - even with this book in your hands and countless more tools - the decision not to atrophy your car's engine because of your fear is entirely yours. You cannot delegate your fear to anyone. You must take responsibility.

I will repeat it because I know we all need to hear it, "we are not alone, and all of us who are alive had, have, or will have fear."

There are many people who are surprised because it seems they have never harbored fear. An excellent example is Martin Luther King. He was a religious man who dared to stop the segregation suffered by the African American population in his country. He raised his voice along with a good number of people to fight for civil rights and managed to get African Americans to be able to vote and improve their working conditions.

Throughout his struggle, he received threats and continued walking, went out and preached, spoke about topics that had been forbidden to him, and Martin Luther King never gave up. He won many awards, including the Nobel Peace Prize. Unfortunately, in the 1970s, he was assassinated.

Another person who also did not show her fear was Mother Teresa of Calcutta. Her life was one example after another of dedication, simplicity, and love. She decided she wanted to help the poorest of the poor, and with this vision, she left her native Albania to become a missionary in India. Sorting through bureaucratic matters and obtaining the necessary permits, she founded her own care centers for street people, for tuberculosis, leprosy, and other highly contagious diseases, and for needy children.

Mother Teresa of Calcutta said that what she and the members of her congregation did was not heroic. She claimed that anyone with the grace of God could do it.

She was an active and unstoppable woman who achieved what she set out to do because she put her whole heart into it. Like Martin Luther King, she also received the Nobel Peace Prize.

She passed away in India due to cardiac complications; she was over eighty years old and still tended to the needy. She was quickly beatified and canonized. Without a doubt, her legacy is one of the most impactful of the twentieth century. Martin Luther King, Mother Teresa of Calcutta, and many others seemed to have felt no fear. They were tenacious and dared to do what they wanted to do. In the two examples discussed, we have talked about religious people. They felt that deep faith and strength from the company of God.

There are also hundreds of examples of people distant from religion who were able to control their fear because there are no beings who do not feel it or who are frightened to follow their vocation. Rather, there are incredible subjects who use their fear to bring out the best in themselves.

How can we use our fear? First things first, you must name it. Throughout our lives, we are going to experience and feel many fears. Some of them are based on lived experiences, and others are not. The fears we feel can be classified into real and perceived. Before explaining each one, I want to clarify that both types of fear are real because they are emotions; therefore, although we do not understand the fear that someone else is living, we cannot discredit it just because we do not understand it. That fear is real and is happening. It is a package of emotions and feelings in the process; it is very important to feel it and learn what we have to learn, then overcome it.

The inherently human fear arises from experimentation and personal experience. This is the fear we call real. The memory of pain keeps us on the sidelines of a risky situation. If I don't pay attention while running, I can fall; if I touch something hot, I might get burned. Animals also possess this fear, as it is the package of emotions and reactions that allow species to prevail.

However, as we grow and learn to survive, another type of fear emerges. It is also anchored in what has been lived and experienced. It is the type of fear that limits us to having romantic relationships for fear of having our hearts broken. It is the fear that makes it impossible for us to commit ourselves because of a myriad of hypothetical circumstances.

This is the fear that turns us into a Chihuahua dog. The first type of fear, the so-called "real fear", involves knowing well our dimensions and our characteristics to navigate the risky situation. That's why it does not deform our own personal perception. How do I use my legs to jump better and not fall? How do I take advantage of my speed to have more fun?

The second fear does change the idea we have about ourselves. The fear of rejection in a job interview can diminish you. You might imagine yourself as a ridiculous Chihuahua dog in a tie, waiting on a chair for the recruiter to attend to you. This type of fear invades your head and diminishes you.

The first fear is quick. It is felt laconically. It is the type of emotion for which one is grateful because it increases our adrenaline levels and makes us act. This primary fear is disposable after having fulfilled its function. This fear shouts at us and alerts us.

The second type of fear, "the perceived," nests in us. It remains subtly in our mind and whispers to us, speaks softly. Above all, it establishes that it is not going to go away suddenly or miraculously. It is the type of fear that necessarily involves dialogue and reflection.

Which of these two fears do you think is more exhausting? Which of these two do you think is necessary?

The first arises from real events that you have experienced or that someone else has lived and told you about. They are life lessons to take care of and protect ourselves. They are the messages of fairy tales and fables: "Be careful if you enter the forest because it is a dangerous place"; it is a fear of conservation.

The second fear, which I call "perceived," also arises from experience. In fact, it is so flexible that it also has its roots in events that have been told to you. You don't have to have lived a romantic disappointment to fear commitment, for example. It is the fear whose favorite phrase is: "Anyone who gives their heart to someone always ends up badly. I better not give it".

It is the fear of the unknown, the fear of hypothetical issues; above all, it is the fear of not knowing how to solve the situation we will be in. They are those much-mentioned crises of the thirties, forties, or fifties; you don't know how you will deal with what is expected of you at a certain age, and you freeze. It is the fear of starting and not knowing how to finish.

The most curious thing about perceived fear is that it is antagonistic to the natural course of a life project. Perceived fear is opposed to the human characteristic of building daily, of not being unfinished individuals.

What fears do you have?

In this book, you will be forced to dialogue with your fears to analyze them. You will have to gather the courage and energy to do so. First of all, you must identify your fear and name it. I want you to decide to face it and embrace this madness called freedom.

You will no longer be the hostage of your fear because you will be able to properly dimension it, to take distance and perspective, to visualize it as it is. You should not fear that your shadow is longer than you, not anymore!

Throughout this book, you will discover that the small and defenseless Chihuahua dog that you saw in the mirror was not you but the fear that lives in you. Your fear is barking.

But why is it barking at you?

THE GODPARENTS OF FEAR

Fear is a human emotion, but we've said that before. Throughout our lives, there are structures and schemes that keep these fears alive. I refer to these structures as the godparents of fear.

When I attend baptisms, I like to watch the faces of the parents and godparents. I wonder if they all realize the immense responsibility they are taking on and receiving. Daring to share the parenthood of someone else requires a lot of commitment and dedication. Your godparents are not just there for a photo and to take care of some party duties, not at all!

These people become known as "compadres," meaning they will be the immediate support for the father and mother. Along with them, they will educate in religion, values, and ethics.

From the godparent of the first communion to the one at the wedding, they receive a commitment from the one who chose them. Even in popular culture and outside the religious context, a godparent is someone who guides the steps of their godchild. This term is often used in relationships with drug traffickers or former addicts moving away from their vices.

Being a godparent entails a mutual relationship with a profound impact on shaping the future. It necessitates active participation from both godparents and godchildren, as they mutually influence each other's lives. In this chapter, I want to show you the major godparents of fear that I have identified. Even if we wanted to forget them, we couldn't because they have been in the world much longer than us and are a part of the reality we live in. These godparents have shaped us, and we have sustained them. They need us and our fear to legitimize and continue.

The godparents of fear are:

- Culture

- Family

- Religion

The godparents will build important relationships that will give direction, rhythm, and flavor to your world. They will affect how you think and decide.

Understanding when each of these godparents becomes a limitation is vital to identify how they affect us. I want to clarify that none of these elements are inherently negative or positive. They are systems in which we have grown, and as such, we have the possibility to transform them and extract the best from them.

What Surrounds You

Your culture can be encapsulated in a phrase, or it can expand and build bridges, allowing you to learn and discover yourself, or it can overwhelm you and confine you to a box.

In the culture I grew up in, we were taught to fear animals more than men, and for city children, it was the exact opposite.

I remember walking in the mornings to collect water taking the opportunity to bathe and groom ourselves; it was also a time for fun. We would return home with our containers "brimming with water," hand them over to the adults and then head off to school.

After school, we gathered firewood, partly for cooking and partly because we had no electricity. From a young age, we learned hard manual tasks and techniques for farming and fishing.

My culture taught me that men and women can call themselves so when they master various skills and activities.

Men should be able to farm their own fields, inherited from their father, build their own house, and get married.

A woman proves her "womanhood" by cooking and nourishing a whole family, keeping the home functional and clean, or by becoming a mother.

For both men and women, the cultural environment filters and interprets their world, and we perceive our circumstances based on what culture dictates.

Naturally, culture permeates marital relationships. I was taught that many activities are permissible for husbands but not for wives. For example, a husband can abuse drugs, mistreat his family, and be unfaithful. The wife must endure and not contradict her husband.

She can never leave despite disillusionment, disappointment, fatalism, and depression.

This widespread thinking around the world leads to other dynamics of controlling women, such as female circumcision (which has no basis whatsoever) or arranged marriages where the husband is twice the age of the bride and often a friend of the bride's father. Such is the power of culture. Such is the oppression that many accept daily.

My mother never studied, and according to my grandfather, everything she needed was in her home. He made it clear that cooking, maintaining a house, being a mother, or a submissive wife were not school lessons. So, she had no choice but to align with the culture of her time and place, and therefore, she did not study.

However, she supported me and all my siblings, as well as several cousins, to get an education. Many acquaintances passed through our house whom she encouraged to become students. My mom was always different, and this cost her some family relationships and her social circle.

Culture is shaped and built in the community, but unfortunately, my mom was influencing her culture, not transforming it radically. It took many years to affirm that it is changing.

Our games and entertainment revolved around hunting and gathering. On weekends, the village children would gather and venture away from our homes. The oldest among us was perhaps twelve years old, twice the age of the youngest. We would run in parts but mostly stayed hidden, learning to detect animal tracks.

"Look," someone whispered, "there's a hole."

When we found one, the next task was to approach and put our hand near the opening. We could feel the warmth and discern if an animal lived inside or even touched the animal itself.

Putting a hand in was an act that added fear, uncertainty, and audacity. Fear of encountering the animal, uncertainty of how to react, and audacity to seek adrenaline and admiration from others.

Many of us wanted to prove we dared, but many others wisely observed. If an awake and alert animal resided in the den, you risked being bitten. This granted you the last thirty minutes of life. We all had half an hour to return the child to our village, hoping they could be taken to a hospital as quickly as possible. However, the village itself was more than half an hour away, and a bite was fatal.

We walked closely among the trees. The elders liked to share their wisdom and advised us on what to do in certain cases. Sometimes, they would freeze mid-step and demand silence with their hand. Encountering gorillas was also a real possibility. Regarding what to do in those moments, our parents had instructed us, but we knew it wouldn't be the same the day we actually saw one.

We enjoyed running through the fields, climbing trees, building traps, and testing them. Part of our explorations was also to demonstrate the efficacy of our hunting strategies. We also learned what we should and shouldn't eat. For us, it was child's play; for many other youths, it was tremendous learning that didn't serve them much.

I liked to go out at night to walk, finding it peaceful and ecstatic. The only thing that took me away from the sky and stars was my grandmother.

"Don't look so much at the sky. It's not for that," she exclaimed.

"Why, Grandma?"

"Because God lives there, and if he sees you watching him for so long, he'll know you're challenging him. Look at the ground now!"

Between long blinks and last furtive looks, I said goodbye to the vastness of the celestial dome and the stars. I believed the opposite of my grandmother; so much splendor so much beauty challenged me to observe, analyze, and appreciate it.

"I told you not to look so much at the sky!" my grandmother would repeat.

I had no choice but to fix my gaze on my feet; then I walked.

I wouldn't dare challenge my grandmother's wisdom and hierarchy. If she advised and then ordered me not to look at the sky, I didn't contradict her. That was my culture, and those were the beliefs I grew up with. With that mentality, I came to live in the city with my family.

Everything was definitely different. We no longer enjoyed a house with a huge yard, no land to farm, and of course, our traps and hunting strategies were unnecessary. If we wanted something, we went to the store where the vegetables, fruits, and protein we bought had likely passed through the hands of a farmer and hunter like we once were.

The streets were delineated, and the houses shared walls. On each block, boys and girls played sports, but they could also spend a lot of time inside their respective homes playing with electronic devices.

In Cameroon, we were between twenty and twenty-four million. In such a fragmented and confronted reality, we are understood by acts and not exclusively by words.

Life in Cameroon has long required the adaptability of its citizens. After all, in just one neighborhood, more than thirty languages can be heard. In total, 300 languages from 25 different linguistic families are spoken. On average, a child in Cameroon speaks six or seven languages just to communicate with their neighbors. Seven different ways to play soccer.

You need to understand, express yourself, and speak. You also learned to be open and flexible with your behaviors and diet because going to a friend's house to eat didn't mean just another flavor. It was another gastronomy, another kitchen!

Our city was a true melting pot. If you didn't keep learning, you were pulled by a huge wave of confusion. You couldn't delay in understanding and expressing yourself because there were many people behind you wanting to try.

School was also different, as was the jargon within it. Sports were a common point of connection, although we played them with less ambition than city children.

In our new home, I soon discovered that a latent risk was the people on the street. We didn't know who they all were. The unknown faces spread, creating nervousness among the older ones. We had to be careful of unknown faces, just as we were careful of the holes where animals innocently slept.

This measure seemed complicated to me at first. I wasn't used to observing the "other," the "foreigner," and fear. However, it was the culture that taught me that this was the measure to survive and protect myself. Suddenly, my list of basic rules widened and lengthened. Life in my village was not my life in the city.

We were forbidden to walk long distances or stray too far. They were afraid that the city would consume us and not know where it would spit us out. But we were impetuous youths. Many of us remembered the cold night wind when we ran under the sky. The darkness in the village embraced and guided us, and we couldn't get lost in such long, open expanses.

"Let's go out tonight," a friend told me.

We were in class, and I was looking out the window. From time to time, I returned my eyes to the notebook so as not to challenge anyone.

"What do you say?" I asked.

"That tonight we'll go out running. Do you want to come?"

I thought of my mother, who would naturally be upset if I broke her rules, but I also thought of the air, the impact on the ground every time I lifted a leg, and the friendly memory of the muscle exerting itself.

"Yes, I want to," I replied.

That night, escaping was the easiest thing, and I met up with my group of friends. And we did just as we had planned; we ran through the streets and alleys of the city. We felt free. Like in the village, there were risks we had to avoid: we didn't approach where there were people, avoided some streets, and didn't stray from our neighborhood.

I looked at the sky, at the stars. I was pleased by the vision of the roads, shapes, and delicate schemes traced up there. I was fascinated by that dark landscape, yet so bright.

I didn't notice a dog near me. With the sound of our steps and the confusion of being accompanied, it approached me and gave me a quick and powerful bite.

The sharp pain replaced my joy of being outside and running. I put my hands on my calf – where it had bitten me – and controlled myself not to cry so much. My friends helped me get home.

"Don't say anything because they'll know you were outside," one of them advised me. "I won't say a word," I reassured him. The next day, I hid my wound under the fabric and walked normally in front of my mom. My friends and I had a secret that filled us with excitement. We had broken a rule, yes, but for many of us who came from outside, it was akin to simulating - with a simple practice - that you had been to our place of origin. We felt a similar adrenaline to what we felt in our old home. It was like speaking your own language for many hours without worrying about whether someone understood you. It felt good, really good. Culture also adapts and deforms to make us feel protected.

"How's the wound?" one of my friends asked. "I think it's okay," I replied. I lifted the fabric of my pants and showed them, and immediately, their expressions showed me that it wasn't healing as I had hoped. "Does it hurt?" "Yes," I answered. I couldn't bear the torment for more than two days and had to confess to my mother that I had run away, that we had run through the night streets, that a dog had bitten me, and that I had tried to hide it. I had to tell her that I had dared to gaze at the sky for a long time; I had challenged.

She strived to get me the necessary care to minimize the pain in my leg. There was no more talk or reprimand. My mother didn't have such a strong prejudice against the risk that my friends and I had taken. Like me, she also missed the village and our customs. Perhaps if she had been a city woman, her anger would have been greater.

Cameroon is a clash of cultures, as everyone brings with them what they have learned and begins to live according to it, albeit adapting it to the patterns they discover among their neighbors and other people.

However, a connecting thread among the variety of cultures is the role of women. They are taught to be submissive, not to question, and to take care of the well-being of men. Many women are, and were obliged, after marriage, to stay in the neighborhood or area where the father-in-law lives. The daughters-in-law must learn to please him, to cook or clean for him if the mother-in-law is not there; they are authentic patriarchies.

Where I come from, for example, we learned that only adult men can eat goat meat. Children and women are not allowed, as it is believed that it will make them ill, and women are also not recommended to eat it because it can interfere with their ability as mothers. They cook it but don't taste it, not knowing if it turned out tasty or not.

The reality is that it is a cultural measure established by men themselves so that they can eat more. In reality, meat does not affect children or women, but the cultural weight is so strong that it stops us and continues to stop those who live with this idea.

Culture includes a number of limiting prejudices. Leaving the country, studying elsewhere, living on another continent: all these actions that I have carried out throughout my life can be real challenges or challenges to my culture.

Many believe that because I live in the United States, I have a more peaceful, lighter lifestyle. When I visit or go there for work, they comment on it. "Surely there is not so much hard work there," they tell me. "Let's see, what time do you finish work?" "At three." "And what time do you start?" "At nine." "Do you rest during your day?" "You could say yes. I have time to talk to neighbors and have a drink." I remain silent and do my mental calculations. "I work more hours than you, many more." "Really?" they ask, astonished. "Yes! And I don't have time to talk to my neighbors." We all burst out laughing and continued talking. During the conversation, more and more prejudices imposed by culture emerge. It's their survival mechanism as the godmother of fear.

When I was at the seminary in Chicago, some decades ago, I came across the opportunity to help set up computers. These would be used by us. So, I attended the call. The other attendees were Anglo-Saxon in appearance. They looked at me, and one of them dared to ask me what I was doing there. I know his doubt didn't come from rejection but from curiosity.

For him, it was unheard of that a person of my color knew how to work with computers. I explained that I did know, and we continued. This incident reminded me of the feeling of inferiority that was instilled in me in my country in relation to Anglo-Saxon or English-speaking people. We looked at them as if they were more intelligent and more capable. Above all, they showed a range of possibilities about what to do in our communities and how they could also help us - they were the foreigners, the ones looking for something that we had and that they wanted.

These were prejudices. Culture tends to outline what is allowed and what is not in our relationships with other genders, races, and cultures.

Discrimination, contempt, and distance between the possibility of the other and me are born.

On a flight from Brussels to Washington, we faced very bad weather after crossing the Atlantic Ocean. The winds were very strong, and it was evident that the pilot would have to struggle a lot to land.

A passenger next to me clung to the seat. "I hope she does it well because the pilot is a woman," he said with an ironic voice.

Racism, discrimination, and a myriad of social "phobias" are formed within the cultural framework. We carry so many learnings and beliefs that it is challenging to identify them all and decide whether to eradicate them or not.

I am currently undertaking a project in the region from where I come. We are building a center where teachers and students will be attended to and guided with the intention that neither of these two actors stops dreaming.

We want the children to stick to school and be sure that they are absorbing and appropriating valuable knowledge for themselves. We want their competencies to be similar to those of city children and for them to be able to obtain more and better opportunities through their education.

We seek for teachers to be adequate and human guides for these girls and boys. That they have the training and tools to bring them knowledge and be agents of change from education.

The purpose of this aid center in Africa is to forge sincere relationships of friendship and support among future agents of change in the region.

We will start with a kindergarten and a primary school. In these, Muslim children will converge with Christian children (who are fewer in number).

With this early relationship, it is hoped that when the children grow up, they will not make distinctions but will add to each other to change their realities. The girls and boys will learn that no matter how big the problem is. You can always contribute your grain of sand.

The inspiration for this project has been, to a great extent, my mother. As I already mentioned, she did not study because of the prejudices of her father, but she always supported the rest of us in doing so.

Should we end cultural aspects that limit our development and growth? Should we individually dodge cultural obstacles and fears? What if doing the latter pushes us into loneliness? Accepting what is culturally imposed legitimizes us as members of a society. We belong, and if we decide to be bold and dive into the refusal of our culture, we can die socially. We segregate ourselves, and for many people, denying their culture and accepting new paradigms is impossible. For example, I have worked with many parents who believe they have failed in their upbringing because their children are homosexual. A certain mother once sought me out for advice because she believed that, since she had aborted once, God had sent her a lesbian daughter as punishment. Naturally, this is an egocentric thought because neither the mother nor the father is thinking about the agony of their children. They have been the ones who have mainly opposed their culture. They have also had to live with the rejection of breaking out of the mold and not complying with the social pattern. Being different is a leap for which we are not ready because culture does not teach us to be different. This leap means suspending your belief, your upbringing, your culture, embracing yourself, and deciding that you will no longer hurt yourself by pretending to be something you are not. Denying culture and continuing is an act of bravery. This leads me to what a French philosopher defined as the value of being human. Definitely, you have to have the courage to be human, especially in a world where there are large cultural differences and groups intent on changing minorities, disguising them, and fitting them into the system. If you don't fit into the cultural scheme, you are not part. The fear of loneliness and segregation pushes us to the mental periphery; this way, we avoid the authentic rejection or at least the tangible one.

Those who try to show themselves as they are run the risk of being halfway, neither fully accepted nor fully rejected. What is the individual challenge we face with culture? We must show who we are as unique members, in addition to taking advantage and nourishing ourselves with the best of our culture. Turning what surrounds us into positive characteristics of our personality.

Culture can be transformed because it is something that we build and perpetuate every day with our actions and feelings. Culture, as the godmother of fear can be reconfigured to make us look at new horizons rather than preventing us from seeing the sky.

Influencing or impacting the formulation of culture leads us to another godmother. This one shapes us even more as humans and represents a greater challenge because if culture completely covers us – from head to toe – the next godmother pulses under the skin.

WHAT MARKS YOU

The girl listens fearfully to her father's response. She's bewildered. He has told her no, an emphatic no. She can't study to become an anesthesiologist because it's too difficult and too complicated. "Better to be a nurse. Yes, that's easier and more suitable for women," he suggests. She looks at him, doubtful. She's under twelve, and her big dream is being cut short by her father, his prejudices, and his ideas. Her family structure is not the ideal springboard for achieving what she aims for. The father keeps his gaze fixed on her, wondering if he's doing the right thing. He remembers his parents, who advised him on what to do in certain situations. He feels at peace. For him, the family structure provides security and certainty. A family is like a garden: some are fed with the best fertilizer and watered every day, weeds are kept at bay, guides are applied, and spaces are delimited so no tree overshadows another and no shrub suffocates a flower. But there are also neglected and poorly watered gardens. The sun is fierce against their soil, and no plant grows healthily due to an imbalance of minerals and nutrients. In some families, members can fully leverage their potential and flourish. In others, family members are forced to flee to achieve what they are passionate about and what drives them. The family feeds off other godparents of fear. It is, undoubtedly, the microsystem where each human being develops and begins their process of humanization and socialization. Even if a family member manages to break free from that garden and walk towards other meadows, they will drag their roots; they will fall behind them and pursue them. This person must live with it as healthily as possible. We cannot deny where we come from, but we can define where we are going. Our family reveals the world around us and, in turn, reveals us to the world. From the first cry we emit at birth, we are already marked by genetics; we have relatives and a surname. It's undeniable that we come from someone else. Welcome to the world, welcome to earth. You don't get to choose where to live or with whom. That's already been said and decided by someone else. Culture can change and transform, but various aspects of the family cannot. Our family history will weigh on us and limit our steps while our complete and latent will form in its entirety. I emphasize the family because it's crucial and important. You cannot completely distance yourself from something that lives within you. With families, there are no refunds or exchanges. It goes beyond the complex blood relationship because it affects how we are. It's in the family where we learn to walk, eat, express ourselves, understand, communicate. We will act and behave in harmony with the values and precepts each family has nurtured us with. The family is also a living and integral organism that extends and reproduces. It is defined based on the decisions of the oldest members or those with the highest hierarchy. Depending on how tight the family ties and acceptances are, values can be transformed. It's true that the family is not a static organism; however, it carries various devices that endow it with permanence through time and generations. We are always within a family. Most likely, we often doubt what happens within our nucleus: Should women not study? Should we sacrifice great scholarships and educational opportunities not to separate? Should we accept mistreatment or abuse simply because we are related? A healthy and balanced family relationship is one that does not produce deep and rooted traumas or fears. I frequently interact with fearful people, and it's not surprising to find that the roots of their anxieties or depression originated in their family environments. After all, the family signifies a daily dynamic and coexistence. Unintentionally, we learn and absorb from it. We are one, but also part of the family. Together with our relatives, we form a unit. Yet, more questions arise: To what extent should we respect and uphold it? Is it the task of each person to recognize their family and break with the family pattern? There are many people with deplorable family cases. Many of them chose to distance themselves, to uproot themselves from the garden and leave. They also tried to hide the roots that hung from them and sought new fertilizer for other trees; they planted themselves far and alone, hoping to build something for themselves that they, in turn, would want for others. Many of these people who distance themselves and cut all family ties are acting out of their fear. They are denied and blinded by the fears and scars their own family has created. From fear, more fear was born, and perhaps an even deeper and more dangerous kind of fear that segregates. Returning to the question of how far we should respect the permanence of family structures, I want to give an example: the same girl who wants to become an anesthesiologist comes home from school. In the living room, in the kitchen, and in the rooms, a cold silence reigns; her skin crawls, and she knows what this means. She drops her backpack and almost immediately hears a moan of pain. She knows her father is hitting her mother again. She knows it all too well. Then there are screams, nervousness, more pain, and a lot of crying. She remains frozen next to the door. She doesn't know what to do because the times she has tried to intervene, she can't stop the blows. It's even worse because her mother receives more. She doesn't know what to do right now, but she knows that in the future, she will strive with every pore of her skin, every synapse of her thoughts, and every tear of her body to eradicate this type of violence. She will try to stop men like her father, who do not respect mothers, daughters, or women in general. This girl has detected a great vice that she does not want to inherit or reproduce. She will not have to act with her father's insecurity nor get another person with misogynistic thinking to be her partner. Her family is violent; her father's behavior is lacerating. She wants to leave that garden but not forget how painful the weeds that suffocate other weeds are. This girl wants to reach the spring of her existence and bloom in an ideal garden for it, but unfortunately, we repeat patterns. This girl is more likely to act just like her mother did and start a relationship where domestic violence exists. She can easily become the member who flees and repeats what is killing her internally. So what does she need not to repeat the pattern? What does she need to not forget what she detests so much and to combat it? When we stop being afraid, when we confront what is happening to us with the real possibilities of what could happen to us, everything changes. Definitely, nothing happens until we allow it to happen. Confronting established schemes requires strong discernment, a process carried out in the present with all our intentions and will. This girl needs courage and light. She must prevent fear from growing to be able to leave it behind. I reiterate the family is a garden in which we can intervene and act. It becomes a godmother of fear when it suffocates us and prevents us from creating new paradigms. Many of the internal structures of the family are guided by the next godmother of fear.

WHAT GUIDES YOU

Religion has always been a fundamental element of society. For millennia, communities have striven to find answers, to decide where they come from and where they should go. Religions try to mark a path.

From the Christian belief that God created the world and the universe. God created everything and gave his creation to man to enjoy. This gift inevitably demands a close relationship with the creator.

Over time, religion has adapted and conformed to new social structures. Many religions have modified their doctrine so that the message remains relevant. The ultimate goal of religion is to define the search for the meaning of life and to propose answers that should guide human behavior.

Religion dictates what is right and what is wrong; if we do the right thing, we get a reward, but if we opt for the wrong, we receive a punishment. For Catholics, the reward is heaven (life with God), and the punishment is hell (the absence of God). In heaven, we receive love, and in hell, we live with hatred and fear.

A fundamentalist current of Islam talks about seven rewards that God reserves for those who die as martyrs of the holy war. One of these promises is that the man who dies in the holy war will receive seventy-two virgins in heaven. The holy war includes killing infidels (non-Muslims) because they do not do God's will. The more "bad" people a Muslim fundamentalist kills, the closer he will be to reaching heaven with the expected virtue and reward.

Where does such divine will lead them? Many opt to plant bombs and die along with their innocent victims. They are people who die with the strong conviction of fulfilling the desires of their god.

What God wants, what God asks of you, God's will. This is a topic that has been distorted many times to comply with the schemes of fear. When some elements of religion are twisted to force you to give up part of your freedom, religion becomes a godmother of fear.

Why have we been taught that everything that happens to us is God's will? Religion can be perceived as a system designed to achieve the purest and most real happiness. This interpretive code of life proposes to guide us towards the fulfillment of our humanity. We will be happy and fulfilled people if we follow God's will. This is what religion tells us. Along this path, there will be many threats; there are sacrifices, pains, temptations, and the possibility of freezing in fear of offending God.

Many people are inculcated with the fear of God in a wrong and exaggerated way. They are men and women frightened of offending Him, of doubting His will.

Thus, there are cases of women who endure their husbands' abandonment because they believe it is the life they are meant to live and that God has ordained it for them. There are also examples of individuals who do not dare to break paradigms because they have been scared of divine punishments. There are even many people who accept violent and inhumane situations with the justification that "this is what God wants for them."

In many cases, the fear of offending God is a fear imposed by the manipulation of religious discourse. Even many religious movements abuse these fears to gain economic support. It is increasingly common for groups that "sell" miracles. They propose to pray for you to get such a job but in exchange for a percentage of your salary. As long as people continue to doubt their ability to solve their everyday and ordinary needs, false prophets will enjoy success.

When religion claims our freedom and poses as the administrator of our lives, it is very easy for it to become a godmother of fear. I dedicate myself to studying and understanding more about our faith and vocation. Talking about God is my profession, and I can tell you with total conviction that faith should not be blind. It is valid to question God. It is meritorious to ask Him: "Why is my infertility your will? Why did you take my baby away? Why should I trust you when you gave me and then snatched away someone I loved and longed for so much? Why are you doing this to me?"

The circumstances of our lives sometimes prevent us from assimilating certain representations of God.

For a teenager sexually abused by her father or an uncle, it is difficult to understand that God is like a loving Father who always protects us.

When Karl Marx said that religion was the opium of the people, he was labeled as diabolical. However, it is more malignant to decide to steal the dreams of your brothers and sisters. It is worse to deceive and lie using God as a standard. Religion should shed light on the questions instead of causing darkness.

"To those who are ignorant, teach them all you can; society is guilty of not providing free education: it is responsible for the night it produces. This soul is full of shadows, and there sin is committed. The guilty one is not the one who commits the sin, but the one who creates the shadow." Víctor Hugo

Many within Catholicism live with a deep sense of guilt and fear of the consequences of their mistakes. The resignation and submission of many people are explained by this logic: "You don't deserve it because you are bad. You are a sinner. Pay for your mistakes and your guilt." Such a feeling drives several people away from an active spiritual life and weakens their faith. Let's use the biblical example of the blind Bartimaeus, who wanted to approach Jesus to be healed. One day, when Jesus was passing by the street where he was sitting, Bartimaeus began to shout Jesus' name to get his attention. Many people asked him to be quiet, but he shouted louder. His continuous attempts, his shouts, and his eagerness caused Jesus to ask him to come closer. Bartimaeus decides to surrender completely and throws away his cloak, which was probably his only asset, and approaches Jesus. The first step towards freedom for Bartimaeus is to face his fear. The biblical text says that he got up and walked towards Jesus. Bartimaeus knows what he wants and, therefore, overcomes his fear when approaching the Messiah. For his faith and courage, Jesus grants his wish. Bartimaeus regains his sight. This story shows the other side of religion, contrary to its role as a godmother of fear. Faith invites discernment and action.

Many people ask me if it is true that religious people are less afraid. It's a complex question, and there is a bit of everything. Just as there are countless believers who live their lives with joy and courage, there are also a large number of people fearful of the consequences of their actions and of their "destiny" due to religious norms. The level of maturity of faith is a determining factor in evaluating the relationship between religion and fear.

Faith is nourished by information, facts, and actions to consolidate itself. I once read an article written by a pilot. In the text, he explains everything from how the flight is prepared to the moment the plane takes off the runway. It was a detailed explanation of each step, each protocol, and each prior action. The last part, however, said that after all that preparation, after the plane is driven and the reactors are pressed to the bottom for takeoff, there is nothing more to do than to have faith that the instruments will work properly.

The pilot who wrote this article stated that one must have faith that the miracle happens so that a machine of more than 300 tons rises above the runway and flies, reaching speeds of a thousand kilometers per hour and altitudes of eleven thousand meters. It is because of so much information and knowledge that mature faith suppresses fear. Obviously, the pilot also knows the risks involved in the feat of takeoff. He knows that if something doesn't work, he is in great danger, but he is also watching the dashboard to see that everything is developing properly.

This type of faith contrasts with the highly romantic vision that has been shown to us of religion in which God is in charge of everything, and anything that happens is at His mercy. This vision forces a crucial doubt, anthropologically speaking: if it were true that everything is the work of God, then why is there so much suffering and inequality? Why do such inhumane things as abuse, evil, and rape happen? How to understand that God wants this for us, His creation? Believing that everything that happens is the work of God is a vision that absolves the human being from what happens around them. Believing that evil exists because God allows it is a limiting and paternalistic perspective. After all, God made us free.

If you belong to a religion that oppresses you with rules and punishments, it is most likely that your spirit is not growing. As human beings, we are intrinsically spiritual and do not limit ourselves to thinking about what we are going to eat but why we are going to eat it. We want to know the causes, observe the farthest stars in the sky, and understand a part of ourselves that lives in others and vice versa.

Religions help us understand ourselves and what surrounds us. However, the foundation and essence of several religions have changed over time because they form elites and power circles. Power can corrupt and be destructive, especially when it is centralized in the hands of a few. There are many historical examples where the immense level of corruption reached by some religious systems and their dark repercussions are palpable. The Inquisition is a chapter of Catholicism that many people still cannot forget or forgive.

Naturally, times have changed significantly, and religions have evolved in the presentation of their message. Different belief systems create connections with their followers in various ways, but the human vices of some still prevail in the treatment of certain minorities or certain behaviors. Homosexuality, for example, continues to be a thorny issue within most religions. The repositioning of the female figure can sound taboo in certain religious circles. To the extent that religion encourages us to be better, it will make us freer and happier. Better neighbors, friends, parents, mothers, brothers, students, leaders, and entrepreneurs. Simply striving to be better people will guide us to freedom and happiness. When we understand, without a doubt, that God has given us the necessary elements to be happy and supportive, to serve others and to unite as a true church, we will have the courage and certainty to embrace the tasks that we face in the circumstances and vocation that correspond to us.

For the journey of life, God has given us qualities and resources, useful tools to behave faithfully to what we are. So why, if it sounds so easy, do few achieve it? Because religion can act as a fierce godmother of fear and limit you. Starting a project of single parenthood is frowned upon; divorce is considered a sin; certain activities and thoughts are condemned by other believers, but also by God?

Have faith because the system might close its doors on you, people might criticize you seriously, certain "concessions" might be withdrawn from you, and they might scare you with hell, excommunication, and exclusion. Arm yourself with courage because God did not create you to endure blows, trampling, or mistreatment; you are not here to be someone else's slave nor to satisfy the system. Religion should convince you.

This conviction comes from an open dialogue between the person seeking an answer and God. If religious systems focus on controlling people's minds, then it evidently becomes the opium of the people. This allows perpetuating power in the hands of a few over the masses. The religion that preaches with fear should not convince us. Convince yourself with the religion that forces you to dare; with the one that grows in your intimacy, the powerful faith and hope;

with the one that makes you project yourself in what surrounds you, having the sky as the limit.

We will always feel some kind of fear. If we think of people who have impacted the course of history like Gandhi, Martin Luther King, Nelson Mandela, Mother Teresa, and Cesar Chavez, we realize that all of them did feel fear. Despite this, what they had in common was that they overcame their fears and their limits.

Religion should convince you that you are greater than you perceive, that there is something more, and that the answers have a certain sense and a certain time. True spirituality is what shapes us as a more solid human being with fewer fears.

An Extensive Network: The Subsystems of Fear

If society, family, and religion were the only godmothers of fear, human situations would be much simpler. Much more so. However, each of these godmothers entails subthemes or subsystems that make the path to happiness and freedom more difficult. Work, mass media, friends, and social networks are some of the subsystems we will discuss. What is alarming about all of them is that they are overly related to our everyday lives. Who doesn't work? Who doesn't have friends? Who doesn't check the television and their social media profiles? They are over and around us. Technological algorithms have reached such a level of sophistication and knowledge of our habits that they know perfectly what to show to each individual. Currently, traditional mass media have merged with social networks, making it very easy for the owners of the media and networks to make a certain figure or a certain news item trend. Everything is calculated, no matter how minuscule it may seem. Friends and work, along with family, are what absorb most of our time. With our professional duties, we have a schedule contract that we cannot break; with our family, to a certain extent, there is some obligations like specific dates when we must get together; but with our friends, everything is different: we want to socialize with them because we chose them.

Tell Me Who You Associate With, and I'll Tell You Who You Are

Imagine two teenagers walking through a shopping mall. This is a common image we all can recall. Picture them however you like. They are two cheerful girls wandering from store to store. They try on clothes, buy something for lunch, and continue walking. The topics of conversation never end. Together, they are forging a strong intimacy and a collective universe that includes their perceptions, definitions, and explanations. Each is allowing the other into what they truly are. Since they have chosen each other, they believe they have made the right decision. They are best friends and share everything: "Did you study for the Arithmetic exam?" one asks the other. "No, I don't plan to. I'm terrible at it, I don't understand anything. I intend to say I'm sick that day and not attend. I just don't get all those rules and numbers." The first friend looks at her in perplexity. Arithmetic isn't her favorite subject either, but she knows she at least has to try. "You can't be like that. Take the exam. That's better than not doing it." The second friend quickly responds. "I'm going to fail anyway. It makes no difference whether I take it or not. I don't know why you're so calm. You're not very good at Arithmetic either!" That simple phrase acts like a fertile seed, growing fear in the first girl. She wonders if her friend might be right; after all, she has never gotten a high grade in Arithmetic. Perhaps unintentionally, the second girl has poisoned the first girl's thoughts. She does it so easily because they are best friends, and both fully trust what the other says. Certain friends make us waver and doubt; they share their panic with us and induce inaction or the loss of our potential. Some friends make us reconsider decisions we were completely sure of because if it's my friend, who knows me so well and wants the best for me, who doesn't support my plans, surely they see something I don't. Friendship is one of the most basic and common relationships among human beings. It implies trust and closeness. It's a free choice because we choose our friends. However, this can be a self-interested choice. Many people choose their close circles based on the benefits these people can provide. From school, we identify those who want to join the so-called "popular" group simply to belong. That is a free choice but not based on interests or values, just on supposed privileges. I have always believed that you and your friends should share tastes. It's much easier for someone who likes reading to find good friends in a book club for an athlete to build good relationships within an athletic team. Our friendships are so important because calling someone a friend means a lot. It's someone who can protect you, who defends you, who makes you feel safe, and with whom you can express yourself openly. It's essentially betting everything on someone with the hope that they won't let you down. It's during adolescence that we learn a lot about friendship, how to make friends, and the type of friendships we would like to develop. Coupled with the complex changes we are experiencing in our bodies, we must deal with the comments of our parents and older relatives. They try to guide us on who should be our friends and who should not. It's also a complicated age because teenagers want to try many things and, in most cases, it's their friends who help them achieve it. However, toxic friends are not an exclusive issue of adolescence. While drugs may be a red flag at that age, during the young adult stage, there are issues like infidelity, work attachment, and independence where our friends can transfer many of their fears to us. It's important to choose our friends wisely, but perhaps it's even more important to strive to be an excellent friend because that can change the entire world. If your friends are fearful, speak with fear, and live with fear, it doesn't mean you should distance yourself. As a friend, you have privileged access to their universe to convince them to abandon their limitations and to motivate them. Just as we have no defense against our friends, they have none against us. Your friends can become the godparents of your fears; you can reflect and become the godparent of their freedom.

THEY'RE WATCHING US

Jim Morrison, the iconic vocalist of The Doors, said that whoever controls the mass media controls the masses. Despite so many years since he expressed this thought, it is still a reality.

From a book to a Hollywood movie, mass media form and shape an extensive and intricate system of beliefs and perceptions. The press, radio, and television were the main architects last century of international stereotypes. To this day, I meet people who ask me if the area where I live in the United States is as hot as Africa. It amuses me because it is never that hot in Cameroon; in fact, being in an equatorial zone, it enjoys rain and high levels of humidity 365 days a year. Africa is not just "the desert near Europe"; it is a very large continent with lush vegetation.

I know that the people who ask me this are based on the concepts about Africa that the mass media have taught them. I have seen, countless times, movies where the place where I was born is dry and where Latin American countries are a huge dump. Neither the first nor the second is true. But how could we know?

It is said that around more than 50 percent of the news we read on the internet is false. Of the remaining percentage, it would be necessary to analyze how biased they are. The mass media are an excellent tool for provoking fear. In fact, according to Naomi Klein's work The Shock Doctrine, using fear as a platform for societies to accept major changes in times of crisis is a technique used worldwide to maintain and satisfy economic and political interests.

Mass media dictate what to do, how to dress, what to think, and what to opine. From the theory called agenda setting, it is explained how we limit ourselves to talking about very few topics because, simply, they are the ones shown to us by television, radio, cinema, the press, and the internet.

It is no coincidence that the owners of television stations worldwide enjoy so much power. After all, they, along with their team, are capable of defining what will happen in the coming years. Mass media are a tool for establishing the parameters of social engineering within regions and countries.

Culture permeates the audiovisual products we receive from the mass media; and a constant question for scholars of Sociology and Communication is: which came first: culture or the mass media product?

Imagine, for example, a Brazilian soap opera. Like any production of this kind, it is exaggerated and dramatic. The cast of characters in this show are a catalog of vices and immaturity. Soap operas are not like Jane Austen's novels where, despite gossip and obstacles for a couple to unite, the characters own themselves and show some development through the pages.

"Typical" soap operas use jealousy, incorrect communication, and a series of usual crimes (murders, corruption, abuses) to take the lives of the characters from bad to worse.

Have you thought of a soap opera? Now think of real life. Do you know any true story that is as intense and exhausting?

Most likely yes. It is also very likely that the real person in the story you know did not dramatize every event in their life. That is, yes, reality can surpass fiction; but the drama of cultural products exceeds the drama of day-to-day life.

What we see in the mass media is exaggerated; part of reality is boosted to the limit, and then it is broadcast. That's how it works.

So let's go back to the question: which came first, culture or the mass media product? Possibly culture. From this, it was started to create, however, what happens when a Swedish woman watches, follows, and gets excited about a Brazilian soap opera? That is not her culture, will she reproduce what she is absorbing? how do the media dictate behaviors and attitudes?

Social networks have been the great tools that certain countries have used to extend their cultural dominance. Just think of countless American movies where celebrations like Halloween, Thanksgiving, Christmas (with Santa Claus as the main figure), and Independence Day are shown, to realize that we know a lot about American culture, but very little about others.

There is also a great example of what is culturally accepted by this country: cohabitation, family detachment, the eagerness for hard work and the accumulation of money.

For many younger generations, American movies, music, and literature have taught them more than school. For example, believing that love "should hurt," that "it should be suffered," and "that it costs" are several bitter lessons that many have believed, adopted, and reproduced because of what the mass media show.

Many ideas that we have adopted as societies also come from radio, television, and the press. Let's think, for example, of the vision that was had of the Russians during the cold war and also think of the number of Russians we know. What we believed were valid tests to prove our point, were not.

I want to give an example of the reach that mass media have when they are exclusively focused on altering public opinion, or the perception of the majority of the population regarding a point.

In 2012, the politician Enrique Peña Nieto became the president of Mexico. His road to the chair was a hidden job for the television stations and the image consultants who positioned him in the minds of people as a pleasant, intelligent, and young man. This project was named "Handcock," and its main objective was for Peña Nieto to win the elections.

The project was exposed months after he had won by British (The Guardian) and Mexican (Aristegui Noticias) media. The investigation presented showed the strategy used by public television stations to improve the vision of the then-candidate. This strategy is not proven by Peña Nieto's Communication team. Who financed such a campaign and for what purpose?

There are even many researchers who mention that his marriage to a Mexican soap opera actress (which took place a short time before he became a candidate) was also a maneuver to get more votes, especially from women.

Enrique Peña Nieto won, and the verdict puzzled several people. Just as there was a large percentage of people who applauded the event, others felt dissatisfied and deceived.

Mexico's case was not extraordinary. Also in 2012, a 29-minute, 29-second YouTube video went viral in an impressive time. In just six days, the video titled "Kony 2012" garnered over 100 million views. The British boy who "Charlie had bitten his finger" did not enjoy the same success. The creators of "Kony 2012" obtained sizable donations, also in record time, 5 million dollars in the first 48 hours.

Genocide, southern Africa, rape, and exploitation of minors. The "Kony 2012" video touched on those taboo issues in first-world countries. It appealed to the deepest and most intrinsic feelings of humanity: compassion, mercy, and curiously, morbid curiosity. However, weeks after its release, criticism emerged from different corners of the earth. After all, how feasible is it to extinguish fire with fire?

At the end of the video, viewers are asked for a donation to obtain a kit of posters, shirts, buttons, and flyers to make Kony famous and to make his crimes known worldwide. They were also urged to take to the streets on April 20, 2012, in a kind of demonstration to governments to capture the African leader. Above all, money is requested for the non-governmental organization that developed this campaign, "Invisible Children," so that they can support the U.S. army, and thus the soldiers can support the Ugandan army and "get rid of" the dissidents.

Joseph Kony is one of the names that appear on the list of the International Criminal Court. He is accused of genocide. According to various reports, he is a being with few scruples and excessively violent. All this is true. However, what is not mentioned in the video is that Kony has not been seen since 2006. For six years before the video, nothing is known of him, or his army, or his acts. Why would an American humanitarian organization need money to look for him?

Yoweri Museveni was biting his nails in his presidential office in Uganda. He had the local media on top of him. He had ordered the killing of 20,000

Ugandans in the name of British corporations. His staunch opponents labeled him as a heartless dictator. Heartless dictator? Cunning dictator?

He could not continue to allow the bad press. He had to save someone in some way. Then he remembered a favor that someone owed him. Something he had kept in a drawer for a special occasion. It was enough to make some calls, and it was ready, from Washington they would help him eradicate a plague of less than a hundred men. The Lord's Resistance Army led by Joseph Kony.

Museveni had supported Obama's army in a war in Somalia against Islamists. The Ugandan president had supported men in the American trenches; the joke was to crush potential terrorists. Evil is rooted out from the root; Washington agreed to the search for Kony. The fact that the International Court gave credibility to the action. Both Obama and Museveni, won. Museveni could continue in power with impunity, and Obama introduced his army into a mineral-rich area. Once inside this paradise, the soldiers' feet turn to lead.

The visibility of Kony, thanks to Invisible Children, justifies the increase of troops in Uganda, 115 in total. That is to say, the initiative of the organization made it known that the army was already "helping," but with the money and support, they could help more.

Thus, the international press applauded the American intervention, and the soldiers were improving communications and military strategies.

However, curiously enough, Kony was not found. One of the most disciplined, professional, and advanced armies went out to look for him under the sunlight, in the lethargy of the afternoons, protected by the moon, and Kony was not found. The favor ended up being collected, and the mass media complied, once again, with the implementation of fear and the blind and poorly informed search.

I leave with anger because my reason and logic did not overcome propaganda, which is the food of fanatics. Suicide letter from Xavier Zaragoza. "The Eagle's Chair" by Carlos Fuentes.

Returning to the controversy around Peña Nieto, since 2012 he had a six-year term of government work with very little acceptance. The same mass media that supported him were the ones obliged to expose that he has been the Mexican president with the least acceptance in the recorded history of the country. With this scenario, the 2018 elections became a turning point. Many voters wanted feasible proposals and a change. In this way, Andrés Manuel López Obrador reappeared on the national scene, a politician who tried three times to be chosen as the president of Mexico. However, with this character and today's current president, traditional mass media was not his only strategy to reshape his perception in public opinion. In recent years, there is a much stronger and better-focused strategy: social networks. I recently saw a report on the fake news agencies present on the internet, whose main showcase are social networks. The owner of these agencies (more than a dozen) congratulated himself by stating that he would be the one to decide who would be the next president of Mexico. He was excited to say that he defined what topic became a trend. Even in the report, he shows that he is capable of doing it. In six hours, he turns any phrase into the most repeated phrase on the interfaces of some networks. This is how the combination of social networks and mass media becomes strong godfathers of fear. After all, we are unaccustomed to looking beyond what is presented to us. Fear grows easily where ignorance abounds. Nothing is more powerful than an idea repeated a thousand times, infected, shared, and gone viral a thousand times. An idea that may not be entirely true, but in its different echoes, with its consequent cacophony, may taste like truth. Mass media have established a gigantic glass dome around us. From this, they observe us, measure us, and lead us. But let me tell you something (before I myself become a godfather of fear) that dome is fragile. It's easy to break it; there is a way out. Be more analytical when reading the news. Check the source and the message. What they are telling you generates something, why would it serve to generate such a state? In the last century, it was believed that the receivers of messages transmitted by social networks were dormant and unthinking entities. There was a theory named "the hypodermic needle" which dictated that the message was accepted without anyone whistling or opposing it. Under this assumption, mass media worked for a long time. Currently, we know that the theory is invalid; we information recipients are not dormant and trained beings. We can transform the message in our hands, we can analyze it and deconstruct it to reach what is truly important. We always have the power of questioning and research. Your curiosity will dissipate fear.

THE INVISIBLE HAND

Norma is scared. She probably should be. She was told that if she didn't join in, she wouldn't exist. No matter how much she complains and how much the idea of being inside a virtual world to "belong" doesn't sit well with her, she knows she will have to do it. She is socially subdued, and it doesn't take a large real army to convince her. The practical and hard arm of the mass media is the virtual social networks. In them, we all fit, but none of us fit completely. The list of options that appears when we click is very brief. "It's complicated," says one of the different statuses; what is genuinely complicated is the way we are forced to be inside. Living life without a social media profile was, until a few years ago, possible. Today it is a requirement to enjoy certain benefits, but also an obligation for other tasks. Certain programs, payments, and services are not accessible to those who pretend to be non-existent on social networks. This is a question that genuinely sows fear: Do I not exist if others don't see me? That's why Norma is scared because she asks herself this question and doesn't know how to answer it. She runs her fingers over the keyboard and opens the most crowded social network, I mean Facebook. She has to create an account to be part of a schoolwork team. She disagreed with the idea but gave in. Few know that a few months ago, Norma had another profile, but with a name and an identity that were not hers. She wanted to know what was happening in the virtual world, but without being discovered. Norma, like so many others, had problems with social networks. If this were a Facebook interface and with a click we looked at the different options in the dropdown list, the problems would include cyberbullying, identity theft, social media addiction, depression due to lack of socialization. The world of social networks is a very delicate and fragile one. Here is where the phrase "a picture is worth a thousand words" comes to life. When Norma was a more convinced and willing cybernaut, she moved the cursor down absent-mindedly. She saw smiles, colors, spectacular hairstyles, beautiful figures, and photo captions with enthusiasm and love. On social networks, people like to show both sides of the coin; either they are "authentically" happy or "authentically" miserable. Norma was one of the people who shared sad comments, blue and tearful emoticons, and slow, melancholic songs. She had friends who traveled, loved their job, adored their pets, and were about to get married. These images, one after the other and arranged in another long and tortuous list, reminded Norma of something; they all have all this because they deserve it and you don't. This message, repeated in Norma's head to exhaustion, pushed her towards a depressive and antisocial state. She didn't realize that most of the things seen on social networks are not real and that the context and feelings of each recipient of the message give it many thousands of readings. In a photo with a woman showing her engagement ring, perhaps someone will see fulfillment, someone else envy, someone else interest. Seeing an endless number of images with such varied meanings is tiring for our mind. It's overwhelming. The other message Norma received was that you should be doing an endless number of things and you can't find a better job or become independent. Social networks become godmothers of our fears when they impose ideas we didn't have before when they make us fit into social conventions that are not our own. There is no age to get married, to graduate, to have children. There is no age or inflexibly established order. There isn't; no matter how many photos and videos you see of people your age who said yes in front of an altar. It just turns out that there are situations that other people have lived and you haven't, or vice versa. Norma could spend hours finding out about other people's lives. Click after click, she would sink into a heavy labyrinth of connections between individuals. She noticed parties she wasn't invited to; comments from people she thought she knew and discovered she "knew" nothing about them. Norma was saddened to compare the life she lived with that of others. This happens constantly: social networks can function as a catwalk or showcase of someone else's idyllic situations. We must not forget that talking about social networks is talking about the ego industry. I remember an article I read a few years ago about a young model who recorded herself telling the truth behind her perfect images on Instagram. She confessed that to achieve that shot, she needed at least 600 attempts. She said she was not comfortable in the photo, nor was she happy, nor did it convey how she really felt. In the same video, she explained how the interactions of social network users with her images made her feel. The hearts, thumbs up, and shows of affection elevated her. She constantly logged into her accounts to verify that they loved her, or rather that they wrote to her that they loved her. But if she stopped receiving positive notifications, she got angry. "Why aren't they talking about me anymore?" she wondered. The audience's silence made her much sadder than their applause. Social networks are a showcase where anyone can get up and pretend to be a scholar, a model, a connoisseur, a guru, an influential person. The style of photos and videos shared requires more attention to detail and more pretense. On social networks, people want to be envied and adored. You are there, or you are not, they adore you, or they hate you, they envy you, or they ignore you. You generate fear, or you are afraid. Social networks have always existed. They are not an invention of this millennium, nor are they creating dynamics. In fact, most of the functions we see on social networks are similar to the ways of coexistence we already have. Being able to share, comment, save information; all these are actions we were already carrying out before. However, in virtual social networks, we are not as free as in tangible ones, in the "face to face" ones. In social networks, we "fit in" and there are more concrete and solid guidelines that we must follow. There's just no other way; we can't modify the programming codes of the networks and do whatever we want. In offline life, yes. With so many rules, so many protocols, so many paradigms to follow and limit, social networks can become a martyrdom for many; just like Norma.

Norma saw images of girls like the frustrated model and believed that her life was sad and hers was not. -Did you create your profile yet?- a classmate asks Norma the next day. -No, not yet. -Don't take too long. We need it now for the task. -It's just that... Norma sighs and decides to be honest with her classmate. -I had serious problems because of social networks. It's like I want to know what's going on in everyone else's life and I can't detach. Besides, it makes me very sad and I compare myself all the time. The classmate looks at her without much surprise. -Did you have Facebook, Instagram, or which one? -Both. -And which one did you use the most? -Instagram. -I thought so. Norma shrugs, not knowing what the other meant by that question. Was that the "human" reaction? -What do you mean you thought so?- asks Norma. For her, it was very difficult to confess something like that. -It's just that I also had problems with that social network. I was very addicted and seeing so many photos also depressed me. Then I read a study that said Instagram is one of the most demoralizing networks, so I deleted it. I recommend that you open Facebook, do the task and delete your profile. You are stronger than all that, Norma. If you keep having problems, there are psychologists who can help you. A couple of friends have gone to therapy for this reason. Norma was very surprised by the naturalness with which her classmate spoke to her about the issue. It's surprising. Then she is not the only one, addiction and sadness on social networks is a recurring issue. More and more people are registering on social networks. Whether it's for socializing, finding a partner, starting a business, or because it's an obligation; more and more are. In fact, if Facebook were a country, it would already have more inhabitants than real countries. 2200 million active users; that's how big it is, and it continues to grow. However, behind each screen and comment, there is a great loneliness on the part of the users. We are there to connect with each other, however, it seems the opposite. So much diversification segregates and marginalizes. So much sharing can be overwhelming. Among those who strive to simulate the perfect life and those who preach that they can't find it, many users face the dilemma that talking to someone is not as easy as clicking a button.

It's a great icy mass that covers the entire universe of social networks. It seems like a sophisticated and unflappable space until an event occurs that certain users label or perceive as "alarming." From there, a chain reaction follows, revealing a complex web of social engineering. Suddenly, not everyone accepts others; they are not so tolerant and close their walls and doors. What we see on social networks is just the tip of the iceberg of a delicate web that can lead us to the darkest depths of society. Are social networks tools? I believe they are. Whoever can read the vast amount of information generated at an exorbitant speed on social networks holds key pieces of how our surroundings work. That day, as Norma returns home, she considers everything she has discussed with her colleague. Being honest brought something very important: empathy and understanding. She didn't have to filter what she said, didn't have to embellish it with other elements. She said it just as she felt it, and it worked. On social networks, we disguise almost everything. Even the "grotesque," the "wrong" has a certain filter. We are also conditioned to the rules of the game that someone else has previously established. Certain content is not permissible on some social networks; other content is not appropriate. We learn that some networks are more visual, others focus more on feelings, others are simply for work. These are mediated, regulated, and legislated connections. They are enormous spaces where we fit in along with the perceived fear that each of us wants to export. Social networks accustom us to feed on emptiness and leave us adrift in an ocean of zero meaning. Norma observes the number of people interacting outside of screens and interfaces on the streets. From her seat on the bus, she joyfully watches the interaction between a woman buying fruit and the vendor at the fruit stand. She sees a group of friends sitting in a café. None of them are checking their phones; most are older. Norma has a slight feeling that the use of social networks has caused a strong phenomenon in her generation and those to come. They have been thrown into the stands of a stadium from which they can behave exclusively as consumers, as audiences, as observers. Some dare to play on the field; the rest analyze them, applaud them, boo them. The interaction doesn't go beyond the stadium. But outside there is another life, other ways of communicating and connecting. There are those simple phrases that haven't appeared in any meme, that don't have any gifs. It's the type of language that each person creates based on who they are. It's the language of those who do not speak with fear, of those who do not even question fitting in, of those who are not waiting for "affection" on social networks. It's the language of the most archaic and long-lasting social networks: the voices of two or more human beings who recognize and dialogue with each other. Even from the bus, Norma feels the displacement that a profile on a social network can mean when not properly dimensioning the use of these tools. There's the risk of staying inside – but outside – observing and feeling through algorithms and other people. It's like observing the sea from a balcony and not being able to feel the sand. As I mentioned before, social networks are simple tools and we are increasingly convinced that they are an elaborate device to understand consumers and achieve more personalized and segmented sales. It is another of the many characteristics of postmodernism, personalizing everything to feel more special and considered. Social networks perform the delicate function of monitoring collectives, groups, and societies. It's no wonder that there are now so many information and data analysts. Like never before, power blocks have at their disposal heaps of information about what people want, long for, and need. For this reason, social networks, along with mass media, can become an invisible watchdog that leads us in what to do and how to behave. It's what suits them best, and they even make us believe that it's also positive for us as an audience. Who is guiding us, and why would they design our steps like this? Norma has an idea. She knows it can be very risky, but she's determined to do it. She wants to prove to herself that fear will not control her again. Her colleague is partly right. The use of social networks should not be limited by our social fears. The anxiety, depression, and envy they generate should not be the motivations for closing accounts. Norma would like to show herself as she is without the fear of not fitting in. She will be authentic, not in the manner of social networks where even the most creative pass through certain filters, scruples, and prejudices before posting something. Norma wants to try to go against the current and share something not simply for the feedback she might receive. In front of the screen, with a rhythm in her breathing that denotes her excitement, Norma writes on her new profile - "Hello, I'm here" -. She posts it without saying anything else and walks away from the computer. Many kilometers away, someone receives the message as if it were a very old scroll inside a glass bottle. This other person found it and is moved by the spontaneity and veracity they believe to read in the message. We are here, we accompany each other, and we are not afraid.

The World According to Your Fears

"Excuse me, do you have any availability?" The clerk looked at me with a comically tender smile. Surely, he was asked that question quite often. "No, I'm sorry. Our next reservations are for the end of 2020." I returned his knowing smile and went back to my seat. We were in a pilgrim's house that also offered restaurant services. It was a very cozy place and, even though we already had lodging, I wanted to inquire about it.

We were in Israel. We were a large group of people eager to understand where Jesus Christ was born, where he was raised, where he had traveled, and – of course - where he had died and risen on the third day. It was a trip we had planned well in advance, and as the departure date approached, the number of attendees dwindled. More and more doubts arose over time: Will they let us in? Is it too dangerous? Is there a risk of being hurt by a bomb? Will we return?

"Did you see the news today?" one of the potential pilgrims on our trip asked me. "No," I replied, "what happened?" "It was terrible. Another bombing in Israel, I don't know, this war is very difficult. Do you think that..." This was the type of question we constantly asked ourselves before the trip. When you don't perceive a situation as possible, you don't even assess its danger, but we were getting closer to the departure date, and many pilgrims were becoming increasingly scared. In the end, only those who genuinely wanted to go and managed to overcome their fear went.

"I think we'll be perfectly fine," I told the person asking me about the news and bombings. "Really?" "Of course. Have faith."

I was leading a group of people from the total number that were going. I decided that we were going to go and that everything would turn out as we had thought. Partly, the positive excitement of visiting such countries outweighed the news I heard about the difficult military situation between Israel and Palestine. And after so much planning, we were in that pilgrim's house, finding out that despite the bombs, shootings, and cruel times, the place had no availability until 2020.

There were tourists from many parts of the world: Mexico, Russia, the United States, India, Germany, Uganda, and the list went on. There was chaos among the sum of different believers and devotees who wanted to attend temples, mosques, and synagogues. Among the streets, people of many beliefs and nationalities were found. I was continuously struck by the strong devotion and faith; and the fact that wanting to know and understand God better attracted so many people.

In the tourist spots, in the guides and expeditions designed for those who want to know the cultures that mix in that part of Asia, there is an atmosphere of much attention and certain alarm. Of course, tourists are not ignorant of the conflict they are in. However, they are not paralyzed by it.

For Jews, Christians, and Muslims, Israel is the sacred and holy land of the Bible. After World War II, the United Nations decided to divide the geographical territory of Palestine and form the first Israeli state. This led to various wars and conflicts between the Arabs who had lived around Israel and the Israelis. After all, the UN's decision meant taking part of its territory from Palestine to form a new country. That's why, to this day, there is a strong battle for the land. The measures both countries have taken have reached high levels of cruelty and pain. It's a regrettable fact because the location they are in is one of great wealth and beauty. Both countries have their arguments to "defend" their territory or try to make their decision prevail over the other.

All these aspects were what my travel and pilgrimage companions feared. I constantly repeated to them that we would be fine as long as we kept our plan and ambition in mind. When we had to travel the highways, some people got scared. It was noticeable inside the car that the atmosphere had changed, but they were alert. "Focus on why we came. Have confidence that we will be fine. It would be very rare to have an accident, so don't worry." My words worked, and I managed to prevent them from having a special apprehension about being stopped. I told them that would be very unusual. This communication with my group allowed us to do what we had to do. We learned, enjoyed, and nourished ourselves from the places we went to. When our journey in Israel ended, and we got on the plane, I stretched out in my seat and prepared for the hours of flight. We had finally passed the procedures of documenting luggage and presenting passports. The adventure for the cradle of our religion was over. I looked out the window and analyzed the sum of feelings I had had in the past days. Surprise, admiration, fear, faith, confidence, and now all this would change because I was returning to my office, my job, and my home. I know very well that I know much more about the place where I live and, therefore, am much more aware of the problems and fears that govern those streets. I definitely don't know Israel in the same way, let alone the strip closest to Palestine. In that area, the deals with tourists, the feigned peace, and the euphemisms that allow thousands of people to visit the Holy Land every year vanish.

From the heights, I wondered what it would be like to deal with fear constantly. I want to share the following life story to exemplify that fear is formed by people, not circumstances.

"I'm not going to lie and tell you I'm not afraid, but I always try to control that fear because I need to keep fighting to reach my goal." Ahed Tamimi, a Palestinian activist.

In December 2017, Ahed Tamimi was detained by the Israeli army. She lives in an area of the West Bank and, like her parents, is an activist and defends the rights of Palestinian children. Just a day before her detention, U.S. President Donald Trump recognized the Israeli state and, therefore, the illegal occupation that this country was carrying out against Palestine. In fact, military elements arrived in the backyard of Ahed Tamimi's house to occupy the area. The same day that Trump recognized the Israeli state, a cousin of Ahed was injured with a rubber bullet in the head. The shooter was an Israeli soldier against a young

Palestinian in an illegal occupation. The impact sent the boy to the hospital and affected his brain activity for life. The young man was at a demonstration against Trump's decision. That Friday is called "Friday of Rage." Hours after the bullet, Trump's decision, and the collective anger, soldiers entered the backyard of Ahed's family home. She and her cousin confronted the soldiers. They kicked and slapped them, Ahed's mother recorded it and shared the video on social networks; the soldiers didn't even report the incident to their superiors. The video went viral. For Israelis, it was a clear demonstration of the honor and courage of their soldiers, who did not react to the kicks and slaps. For Israel, Ahed and her cousin were heroines who were not afraid and managed to show their courage and anger at the occupation. Due to the incident, Ahed Tamimi was detained the next day and spent two months in jail while being sentenced. The non-governmental organization and globally known for its humanitarian work, Amnesty International, quickly came to ask for Ahed's freedom. After all, she was a minor, and the twelve charges she was accused of were hardly provable due to their subjectivity - "aggravated assault," "impediment of military work." Three universal rights were nullified: the right to free expression, assembly, and peaceful association.

The trial was resolved behind closed doors until March 2018. Initially, the charges carried a sentence of up to ten years in prison. However, the verdict was eight months. Naturally, this event sparked multiple reactions worldwide. Yet, the crucial point of Ahed

Tamimi's actions is based on powerlessness, injustice, and courage. Since 2009, she and her family have been organizing demonstrations in their village because Israeli soldiers were blocking passage on the occupied lands where Ahed's home is. Ahed Tamimi states that Palestinian children dream very differently from other children. They don't aspire for toys or clothes but long to get to class without being detained, and if detained, to return home. Ahed Tamimi is not an isolated activist. The daily actions she undertakes to highlight the abuse her people endure are replicated by more young activists; a generation forced to shape itself from fear, with fear as a foundation. However, her perception is quite different from that of another seventeen-year-old girl. Fear cannot be subtracted from her daily life. She lives in a state of war, with occupations and illegal courts determining where she can and cannot live or move. In fact, the video of Ahed slapping the soldiers is not her first encounter with them. In 2012, she was recorded threatening a soldier; in 2015, she attacked another soldier trying to assault her brother. Ahed's decision is simple: she either dares or dares. Above all, the meaning she has given to her struggle weighs much more than her fears. After all, regardless of her age, she perceives the change she can achieve, and this is what drives her. For now, Ahed continues her activities as an activist; fighting for the freedom of her family, neighbors, and fellow countrymen. Unfortunately, the collective efforts of Palestinian activists have not succeeded in changing laws or regulating peace and well-being between Israel and

Palestine. It remains a ruthless war with a thousand interests involved. Yet, the efforts and actions of brave individuals seeking a state of peace for the majority serve as strong legacies and examples of decision and will. When justice and hope prevail in a person, their voice cannot be silenced.

ARE YOU DOING YOUR HOMEWORK?

We all have a mission; to lead a dignified and happy life. Of course, happiness and dignity are two deep and complicated concepts to absorb. Both are subjective and abstract. Will I be happy if I do what the majority tells me to do? Will I feel fulfilled if I get a car, a house, and a model family? Both questions are hard to answer with a single response. Even so, it's easy to notice when a person is truly happy and fulfilled. They radiate a different kind of light, and you realize that these people are not looking to have but to be.

Fear causes instability; initially, owning situations, things, and people makes us feel "better" and "more protected." Fear will push you to have, to accumulate, to take refuge in things and more things. Mainly, the godparents of your fear will try to block access to precise and necessary information. They will numb you with facts that scare you, they will freeze your will. Fear can lead you to the absurdity of not wanting to live life fully or living life without really living it.

An important step in fulfilling your mission is to become aware of your perception of the world and what surrounds you. This perception will define your reality. Taking the example of activist Ahed Tamimi, for her, the piece of land she is fighting for is her history, her heritage, her lineage, and her great love. Only if she can perceive the physical place where she lives in such a way does she dare to fight for it. For her, the reality is that her people have been illegally occupied and that such occupation hinders the daily and necessary tasks of the inhabitants of that region.

This reality may be different for one of her neighbors who perhaps sees the occupation as incipient progress or the ability of their culture and nation to mutate and change its forms.

When the godparents of our fears manage to alter our perception in such a way that they change our reality, it is very difficult to do our homework. After all, paralysis, panic, and fear do not move us towards freedom, happiness, and dignity. They move us towards conformism and blindness.

How could we shield ourselves or inject ourselves against collective and unreal fear? How could we distance ourselves from the godparents without this meaning becoming a hermit?

Your best tool is you, and if you want to protect yourself, you have to trust in yourself, wholly and completely. This means that you must know yourself well, you must reconcile with the person you are and accept it with its virtues and flaws.

Like everyone, you will have your life story that makes important decisions in your life difficult or easy, but if you want to stop being in the crowd and value yourself more, you have to accept those wounds as past events and reconcile with them. You must embrace them and forgive yourself for any irreverence or mistake.

Reconciling with ourselves also means evaluating how external conditions are harming us. Inevitably, the political and social situations of the country where we live affect us individually and collectively. However, it's not about how these events disturb us but vice versa. What can we do to counteract them, to turn them around, to use all our abilities to improve that adverse situation?

Remember that if instead of having, you are, you will have the preparation to face injustice and fear. This is one of the social principles of independences. When there is nothing left to lose, it means we have everything to fight for.

Here you are, that is your reality. How are you going to perceive yourself so that fear does not enter?

Remember that fear makes us give up our commitment, our responsibility, and our personal judgment. Fear makes us tremble because it demeans us; it makes us doubt our actions and our intellect. Little by little it lowers the volume of our voice until we accept anything without question.

This is a topic that Naomi Klein addresses in her book "The Shock Doctrine." She makes the association between an individual experiment conducted on humans. The individual was subjected to various electric shocks and reached such levels of vulnerability that they immediately accepted any supposed "solution" to stop receiving shocks. These supposed solutions could mean stripping their will and dignity. However, the person was in such a degree of pain and fear that they felt that any offer proposed was an oasis.

Years later, the same psychological method was applied so that the inhabitants of Chile, who were led to a shock effect, accepted a package of reforms to their laws. This resulted in an extremely high percentage of economic inflation, forced disappearance of civilians, decreased quality of life, and collective chaos.

If the inhabitants had been at a healthier level of perception, they would have opposed the package of reforms. However, they were looking for something to improve their situation and not be so afraid.

Once again, fear drives us to have, but what circumstances and objects does it force us to possess? Are they the most suitable or beneficial?

All you have is yourself. Think that fear and shock turn you into a castaway. You are among the high waves, you have nothing to hold on to, nowhere to rest. Then think that they offer you a poor and tiny boat. However, you must know that this boat may sound like a sensible solution, but you know that if you wait longer if you breathe steadily if you save energy, you will be able to move on the sea, over the waves, and find a paradise island.

You know there is much more beyond what religion, culture, your family, your friends, your job, the mass media, and social networks let you see. You know that all these godparents have permeated your reality. But convince yourself that you only see what you want to see. You only perceive what you think you are capable of perceiving.

So you swim and keep swimming. Along your journey, they continue to offer you other boats, other tiny disposable islands. Miraculous situations are presented to you, and you do not succumb. You are already by yourself what you most need because if you manage to reconcile, accept, and love yourself, you will also understand that the great task you have been given is simply to improve and nourish your spirit in the best way.

You keep swimming, you do not give up, and in the distance, you see that desired island. How would you feel? Happy, fulfilled?

The task is done every day, whether with strokes, steps, efforts, laughs, joy. It is achieved when we avoid fear and assume the responsibility of painting the world with all colors and not getting tangled up in our own fictions.

FICTIONS

You have to prepare rice. Does it seem simple? This dish is versatile and rewarding. In certain cuisines, it's a dish in itself. In others, it's a side or an accompaniment. It can also be the perfect complement to the main dish, so perfect that its absence makes the main dish feel incomplete.

Rice is important. It can be extremely tasty or very simple, and all this willingly to enhance its companion.

Can you prepare a delicious rice? In various countries, mothers say daughters are only ready to marry when they learn to cook good rice. The steps are simple: wash it, put it in a pot with water, and heat it. The amount of time and water is the secret. However, rice is versatile; you can also sauté or bake it. Either way, you must do it with precision so it turns out well: neither too hard nor mushy.

Having said all this about rice, I invite you to prepare one. You are in a fantastic kitchen; you have all the utensils you can imagine and an unlimited amount of ingredients.

Will you use butter or oil? And if oil, will it be olive or coconut? These are important decisions for the final flavor of the rice. Think you've chosen the oil and are cooking. What else would you like to add?

If you decide on chicken, be careful to cook it well beforehand because if it's undercooked, there's a risk of salmonella. In fact, thinking about it, better not cook the chicken. It's dangerous.

You could opt for fish, though fish has bones, and then you should decide to clean it beforehand or risk eating it as is. If you miss a bone, it could hurt your throat. That means fish is not an option either. It also carries a lot of danger.

You could think about more proteins, but each has its risks. Better to opt for adding vegetables. Choose them wisely to balance the flavors so that none limit the other. As you don't have much culinary experience, you prefer not to add any vegetables, and when you think of any spice or condiment, you realize it's too late because the rice is already cooking.

After the decisions you made, you end up with a white and particularly boring rice. It's a rice that tastes of frustration and disappointment. You let external comments weigh on you and decided based on fear. There are always risks; remember that so they don't take over you.

This was a very bland example to explain how some people live their lives. They don't decide to move to a city they love because possibly there's more crime there, or everything is more expensive. Many people don't want to move to a country they've always longed for because they believe it will be very complicated to learn the language or that they don't have the necessary level to do well outside their home.

Another very common and recurrent argument I've heard lately is from young people who don't want to have children because they say the world is very bad and polluted; they say it's not worth it because those children would only come to suffer.

In the same world where there is as much polluting plastic in the sea as fish, public policies are being created to avoid racism and discrimination. If you focus on the first statement, you'll think it's a cruel and ignorant world; if you focus on the second, you'll think we are an inclusive society that seeks the happiness of the majority.

Cruel and ignorant, inclusive and happy. These are all the fictions we construct and create from the reality in which we live. They become more real the more we believe in them and mark how we live our life. With joy, with responsibility, with fear, with hope?

Fictions are personal ideas, but we also form them collectively. They arrive and are forged by both channels. Whether it's an idea we gathered from a godparent of our fears and grew with our perceptions or an idea that was generated in us but found similarities that legitimized it within the collective. These fictions control us and serve to justify our decisions.

That white and boring rice was white and boring because we decided so. However, our decisions would not have turned it into something other than rice. That is, there are inflexible facts. Their nature dictates that they cannot change just because we want them to. What can change is how we perceive, experience, and adapt them.

There are fictions that many people adopt out of mere conformism. These fictions stop us, immobilize us, make us very similar, or make us procrastinate.

What is the great risk of fictions? Imagine a culture whose only dish is white rice. It serves more as a simple side, it's boring and tastes of frustration. Can you imagine it? The risk of fictions and the practices they lead us to is that we walk with our eyes closed, not enjoying everything that has been given to us, and without the possibility of stepping out of that path and doing things differently.

Another risk is that, given they are social conventions, no one will doubt our fictions, nor oppose our justifications. Even if they did, if we are entangled in this thirst for conformism and absurdities, we couldn't hear it.

"Here is where we have to live, and things are not going to change just because we want them to" is an argument reproduced among people who don't strive to earn more, who don't invest more hours with their children to form better human beings, who don't dedicate more passion and love to their relationships, and who don't fully know themselves nor let others know them.

In the end, most fictions boil down to the idea of not doing things because they won't have any impact, or the impact won't be strong enough to change the facts.

Fictions boil down to a lack of confidence and an excess of fears. They are extremely sticky, contagious, and inheritable. By levels, fictions take us from fear to apathy, from apathy to lack of action, and from lack of action to laziness. For the godparents of fear, nothing is more favorable than a group of lazy and hopeless people. They are more manipulable.

We've already talked about having a mission. Apart from that, you have a great responsibility: you have to learn to use the rainbow.

THE RAINBOW

Have you seen a rainbow? Most likely, yes. During childhood, it's one of the most incredible natural spectacles to observe. Whether in a fountain or when the sun comes out after the rain, the rainbow is striking.

Turning to the scientific explanation; the way light refracts when passing through raindrops; we marvel. The world around us is palpable, tangible, measurable, and yet among so many metrics, it's the colors that prevail and make life worth living to see them one more day.

The rainbow is sometimes very precise, other days more colorful. It's never the same, although the phenomenon always deserves the same explanation.

Why do I talk so much about the rainbow? Because, also surprisingly, its definition, the intensity of its colors, and its breadth are in us. Light travels by itself, and passes through water, the rainbow is there, but it's up to us how we see it and how we use it. Everyone has an internal rainbow.

You have the ability to use all the colors, to enhance them, to decide whether to let things surprise you, impact you, scare you, or freeze you.

We have the responsibility not to see things as we are told they are; to use all the colors of the rainbow and analyze what lies beyond.

It's also our responsibility to dare to venture into drawing a novel reality for ourselves, with hope, full of light, and with plenty of space for everyone.

We have been molded based on schemes, and much of the prevailing systems control us with fear and ignorance.

But enough of being stopped, not daring to ask, and perceiving ourselves as that tiny, scared dog. We are not that fearful chihuahua. We are children of God with responsibilities, missions, tasks, and a wide range of tools to achieve them.

What color do you want to paint your day? Which hue will prevail in your life? The one you decide if you dare to silence the godparents of your fear.

Visible Wizards, Real Charlatans.

The day you decide to quit smoking, I'll recommend a great workshop for you to stop completely.

Sitting across the table, Joel observes his aunt. He gives her a fake smile. She believes she is giving him great advice, but that's not the case.

For five years, he has attended courses, bought products, and tried different techniques to quit smoking. Nothing has been effective. He recalls the hundreds of brochures he has read, explaining how a smoker's addiction can be easily eradicated.

That's why he just smiles at his aunt and accepts the proposal. "The day you decide" these words bother him, but he doesn't know exactly why. Ten minutes later, he politely says goodbye and leaves his aunt's house.

He's a 32-year-old man. He has no family, no girlfriend, and not many friends. He is very successful in his job and invests more hours in his professional duties than he would like to admit. He doesn't sleep well, has obesity problems, and is terrified of going to the doctor.

He drives fabulously, is very funny, and likes black and white movies. He smokes about eighteen cigarettes a day. A few years ago, the number was double. He feels happy with certain improvements in his life, however, at the end of each day when it's just his pack of cigarettes and him, he feels overwhelmed. Tomorrow is another day, and he doesn't feel ready to face it.

Maybe it's his aunt's comment or the cold times of the year, but that day, he decides to buy a series of videos that some friends recommended to solve his "mental blocks." Joel confessed he didn't believe in any of that, but he has no pending tasks, and the trendy TV series don't catch his attention.

After a couple of clicks and a bank exchange, he has the total videos on his computer. Bored, he navigates the website interface of the person who will miraculously fix his life. He is the main character of the videos, a kind of coach, psychologist, and traveler who has gathered a group of techniques and questionnaires to "access the conflicts that bind us and prevent us from being ourselves in the fullness of our potential."

For Joel, it's charlatanism, but he will give it a chance. It has been recommended to him many times and with great sincerity.

He pours himself a huge cup of coffee and clicks on the first video. Immediately, the cheerful face of a person running on the road appears. Next to him is an impressive blue sea. This person neither sweats nor seems to struggle. In fact, it looks like he's not even touching the ground. It's as if he were flying as if he were weightless, and no problem subdued him.

"Each one is where they want to be" reads a caption in the video. Joel is tempted to stop the video. However, the prompt intrusion of another voice stops him. On-screen appears the coach who will help him.

"Hello, my name is Ricardo, and if you're here, it's because you definitely have a problem. Am I right?"

Joel is not going to answer. After all, this is just a video. However, he knows he doesn't have one but a dozen problems.

"I want to help you and I can help you. In the next video, we will analyze how to name and face this unresolved issue that is limiting our potential."

Joel is sure the next line might include the phrase "the best version of yourself." He already knows this speech by heart because it's not the first time he's heard something similar. He closes his computer and goes out to smoke. While exhaling the cigarette smoke, he knows he is completely sure of himself. In his opinion, these are miracle products, supposedly magic. He believes they initially work but that the effect is very short. It doesn't last until you really solve your problems. He believes he doesn't need these charlataneries to feel better, does he?

Kilometers away, Ricardo's voice is emitted by a powerful sound system. Those who listen to him are seven older women. All of them smile and affirm every time Ricardo asks them something:

"Is something missing from your life?"

"Yes," they answer in unison.

"Don't you know at what moment you stopped living in the moment?"

"Yes," they respond again.

And the image of Ricardo from the screen again offers them a complete and guaranteed solution to their problems.

These women meet once a week to watch Ricardo's videos and to practice the techniques he teaches them for a more complete life. They haven't realized the huge amount of money they've invested in materials, videos, podcasts, conferences, and products from the system Ricardo created to help people. They even brag about who has bought the most or who among them is the most disciplined.

Two out of the seven women were trailblazers in the realm of personal improvement. Their enthusiasm for their progress prompted them to heed Ricardo's counsel and extend invitations to others to join their group. Like them, there are many other women and men who believe the solution to their problems is a person other than themselves. They trust the resolution and improvement of their life in someone else's philosophy. They buy their remedies, acquire the miraculous benefits of a "holistic" program that, more than anything, is a great commercial product.

Why did the same message work for the seven women but not for Joel? Why did Joel decide to stop the video and instead smoke? Why are there people like Ricardo who have become authorities on personal improvement?

To explain this phenomenon, I want to transport you to a dirty and extensive market. It is covered with tarps and cardboard. When it rains, the water seeps through the plains of the sheet metal walls. The market is located in a poor area of the city. Those who enter these halls filled with merchandise do so carefully and attentively. Maybe they go to the market because they want to buy something, but there's a better chance they'll lose their wallets.

Follow me through this market. As we get closer to the shadowy areas, the products change. They are no longer pans, cleaning products, and clothes for sale. We also leave behind dubious-origin items like watches and perfumes. We continue deeper until we come across little bottles and boxes of vibrant colors. Some are soaps for heartache, others are perfumes to attract money.

We are getting closer to products and people related to witchcraft and shamanism. On a banner, we read words like magic, bonds, and solution. Think, what kind of person would go to a market like this to buy such a product? Do you believe that some individuals think that applying such cream or wearing a certain lotion will fix their lives? What would a person need to accept a solution like this?

Surely that person is very scared. They are very afraid.

We had already talked in previous chapters about the rapid acceptance capacity we have when we find ourselves very vulnerable. If we are scared, doubtful, and with very little information, most likely we will accept any remedy without considering the possible consequences or the legitimacy of the offer.

For many years, the idea that witchcraft solves our problems has been an important topic in many cultures. Not only are the bonds and spells that supposedly can help us, superstition is another way to subtract responsibility from ourselves and distribute it among external elements.

Apart from the archaic procedures that supposedly will give us work, love, and health, there are people who believe they have the capacity to solve our problems. I call them witches and warlocks, although they don't need hats or brooms to be so. They are individuals who sell us answers, who commit to changing our attitude and our habits.

Their mechanisms always follow the next pattern: leave everything in my hands, and I will help you. But what is everything and what does their help really consist of?

In the 1980s and 1990s, several models of peaceful and spiritual coexistence emerged. These were groups of people who, tired of city life, left everything behind and moved to large farms in the countryside. They produced their own food, worked for themselves, and were led by a kind of guru towards enlightenment, balance, and love. These leaders, lacking real and verifiable experience in spirituality, boasted of guiding others to high levels of happiness and balance.

What began as an organic and holistic idea sometimes devolved into unhealthy, abusive hierarchies. Some gurus leading these farms faced serious legal, sexual, and psychological accusations. They created situations of power and trust abuse. The problems these groups initially sought to escape became minor compared to the personal hell many members experienced.

These are extreme examples of the negative outcomes of trusting someone without evidence or reasoning. Initially, these gurus represented a solution to the farm members' problems, offering a different way of life and understanding of the world.

Their ability to easily influence many people is an exceptional power that, in the wrong hands, can cause severe and regrettable problems. Some of these gurus are still hiding, facing long lists of crimes.

There are also large-scale examples of people positioned as problem solvers, attracting followers and more than their time and effort. In the United States, a certain sect amassed a fortune and a large following by extracting valuable private information from believers, making it difficult for them to leave due to exposure and vulnerability. Despite facing serious tax issues, the sect continues, supported by many believers, offering miraculous solutions to people's fears in exchange for their confidentiality and vulnerability.

Like the so-called witches, shamans, and sorcerers of past centuries who had valuable information about those who sought them, modern figures control others using confidential information. The power of blackmail lies in the secrecy another holds over you. Today's "witches" use grandiose words, testimonials, and appearances to gain trust. They appear in moments of vulnerability, using specific information to demonstrate understanding and a desire to help.

Remember, these people are skilled at making you believe they know the problem and the solution. But it's crucial to recognize that fear should not dictate crucial decisions, and responsibility shouldn't be outsourced. The antidote to these "witches" and their miraculous solutions is to see oneself as an informed buyer, not succumbing to charlatans. Realizing that personal decisions shape one's life path empowers one to not need others' intervention.

THE CELL

"My dear,

You and I need to part ways. I can't believe at what point I began to depend so much on you. I can't understand why I feel the need to feel you all the time, to know you're with me, to require you.

We need to separate because what I'm doing with you is wrong. Come on, how much time do I dedicate to you? How many hours am I stuck with you as if nothing else existed?

It will surely be hard for me because I'm used to you. It has happened that you're not there and I hallucinate you. I feel your presence or hear you, even though you're not there.

That's why I'm convinced we need to separate; not completely because I need you for many things, but our rhythm of activities must change.

I'm grateful because you've made me laugh a lot, taught me many things, and supported me in many moments, but if I can't stop my obsession and dependence on you, I will destroy myself. I'm pushing away my friends and family because of you.

From tomorrow everything will change.

"I don't want to depend on you, cellphone."

We don't weigh what the scale says. We have to add the extra grams of the device that's almost always in our hands. Less than two decades ago, a cell phone didn't have the capabilities it has now. Today, it's an infallible work tool; it's a phone, calculator, planner, notepad, sound recorder, dictionary, music and video player, alarm clock, encyclopedia, etc.

Cell phones and mobile phones evolve daily, offering a broader and better range of creative possibilities. This is fantastic, but unfortunately, we don't use them specifically for this.

In fact, we don't even use the cell phone for what it was created for. It's proven that younger generations struggle to make phone calls, wait on the line, and have a conversation with another human being. They prefer to write, send images, or even voice notes; real-time conversation terrifies them because they couldn't express or communicate with the cosmetic elements that hide each individual's specific characteristics.

Younger generations will never understand what it was like to leave home and focus on the present, the tangible, what was happening in front of us in real-time. I remember when we went out and upon returning home, we had to ask if someone had called us, or we listened to the answering machine. Yes! That device that now seems so useless and impractical.

Maybe if a young person is reading this, it will seem absurd. However, the feeling of freedom from not having to attend or depend on a device was glorious. We had much more time to focus on other matters, to reflect, to meditate, to think. Walking was about fixing our gaze on the horizon and moving one foot after the other. Many thoughts came to us and we decided whether to rest or use that time to mull over another issue.

Today, walking is about being aware of the cell phone, of the scenes we come across in case we want to take a picture. It's walking without the ability to get lost and having to ask someone else how to locate the point we were going to. The cell phone also has GPS included, preventing us from getting confused and making a wrong turn on some street. We have information so at hand and "real-time" communication so present, that we no longer need to interact with the tangible world around us.

It's true that smartphones with internet are a window to the world, but they are also a very large window where fear enters. This opportunity to know places, people, and situations that are not part of our everyday life brings with it a ball of fears and insecurities.

Since the era of virtual social networks, many couples have faced problems and conflicts due to the presence of more "subjects" in their relationship. For example, there are many people who sense that some kind of gesture or interaction of their partners with someone else on social networks means infidelity.

For some, it's comical, but for many others, it involves real frustration to be able to keep an eye on the other at almost any moment. What do I mean by these conflicts caused by cell phone use that didn't exist before?

I offer you certain examples:

- People who get offended because their messages were not answered, knowing the recipient already received it.

- People who believe they are being lied to when they are told they are busy but appear "online".

- People who sense that if someone else likes their public message on a social network, it means something more than a simple like or empathy.

They may seem ridiculous examples, but they have become common problems today. Now sharing passwords is a great show of trust when, in theory, a password is meant to keep confidential matters.

The attachment or detachment from cell phones not only generates conflicts within romantic or friendship relationships, it can also be controversial between parents and children when the latter do not answer. Parents worry a lot if they don't answer the cell phone when this can be due to many other things before a theft or kidnapping.

The cell phone becomes a window of fear when it's a total extension of our person; when we deposit our information, our attention, and a large part of our interactions in this device, it becomes a vulnerable point.

-Do you know where my cell phone is?- asks a man of about fifty to his companion. Both are traveling in a car. -No, I don't know. -How can you not know?, I'm sure I lost it! We have to go back. -Have you looked well? The man now turns to the driver and asks him to return to the place where they picked him up. -But are you sure you lost it? -Yes! It's not here, I can't find it. Both remain silent and only the roar of the car is heard. Suddenly the man begins to complain: -This is terrible because there I had some contracts and, my God, so much information and some photos I needed for... -Relax- she says —sure we'll find it. -Hopefully, because I really need it. How am I going to finish that project I told you about? They arrive at the place and the man quickly gets out. She remains in the car. As soon as he got out, she sees the cell phone under the mat of his seat. She says nothing. She waits for him to come back and continues to listen to his multiple complaints. It seems his life depends 100% on his cell phone. -It's a fact. It's lost. Lend me your cell phone to block my accounts. -It's at your feet- she interrupts. He checks and smiles with pleasure. He hugs her enthusiastically and asks the driver to move on. She says nothing. It's not the first time she sees how people get upset when they think their cell phone is lost. Heck, it has even happened to her.

Apart from our dependency and unreal need for the cell phone, other phenomena related to the constant presence of the cell phone have been formed. Many people believe they feel it vibrate or even hear it when this is not happening. Other people sleep with it or always need it with them because they believe they will surely be contacted.

Apart from the need we generate towards the cell phone, we also form a good percentage of our personality with respect to the interactions that only the cell phone offers us. In some people, there is a great difference between how they behave through their cell phone and how they are face to face. In fact, among young people, the way of communicating has changed because they express themselves more as they would virtually than as they would in person.

The cell phone is a great tool, an excellent medium. It is an incredible possibility of creation, design, effective problem-solving, and a perfect way of communication and connection.

Be smart about how you use it. Remember it's a window to other realities, but the things happening around you right at this moment will never repeat. Take advantage of the tools you have at hand to learn more and generate more knowledge.

Nameless Awards

When Beto enters his office, he feels his skin
crawl. He wouldn't admit it even to his wife, but this
moment of his day fills him with dread. With his dark
backpack, gaze fixed on the floor, and about four to
five hours of sleep, Beto opens the door and dares to
walk down the main hallway.

He greets the receptionist with little effort and
tries not to look at the display case. He almost always
fails. Among the collection of trophies and awards his
company has won, he notices the light accumulation
of dust, a thin film covering everything. He also
observes the golden typography and styles from past
decades. The nineties marked the peak of his
company. He can tell, and now almost everything is
different.

Companies try to cosmetically hide the fact that
the logic of competition reigns among employees and
companies alike. They claim it's not about who can
make more sales but the quality of those sales. The
reality is entirely different and ruthless.

Among the trophies and awards, Beto encounters
his own reflection. He identifies the same expression
as yesterday and the day before. He's frustrated and
scared. It's undeniable: he looks like a tiny, scared
dog. Shaking his head side to side, trying to shake off
those features, he walks to his office. Like almost the
entire building, he, too, has suffered with the new

work parameters. Gone are the small, uniform cubicles. Also gone are the spacious, elegant, and private offices.

Now, there are "shared" spaces separated by glass walls. He, as a manager, is meticulously observed by colleagues from other areas. The office has completely changed, even featuring treadmills with screens for working and exercising simultaneously. There are more colors and "positive" phrases on the walls, supposedly to motivate employees.

If Beto takes a call from an important client, he suffers because he knows he's being watched and can't raise his voice. The extent of openness and dynamism is senseless.

Conditions have changed dramatically since younger generations showed reluctance to spend so many hours in a place of neutral colors, where cordiality was the currency. Things were changing. Beto knew it perfectly and wasn't against it. What terrified him was reaching the finish line. He was afraid of not reaching it.

None of the trophies, awards, and other honors in the entrance display case bore his name. Yet they were won because of him. He knew it, his former team knew it, his former bosses knew it. He had been a great salesman and administrator, possessing various skills that made him the best in his field.

Once, his name had become a legend. Bonuses, trips, promotions, and more made up a long list of professional successes. But none of the trophies bore his name. Those recognitions were not for him but for the company he had served for over thirty years. Now, approaching his sixties, he heard the rumors in the corridors. Beto was old and rusty. Too big, too mature.

He heard this from the younger ones, those who envied his position and wanted to climb the organizational chart. From those his age, he heard nothing, nothing at all. They were no longer there.

In fact, Beto was one of the company's longest-serving employees and also one of the luckiest. The fate of his ex-colleagues had been very different. Many were laid off just before their fifties under the excuse that their position no longer existed. Others were even forced to sign their own resignation. Illegally, they were disposed of because they no longer generated the same percentages as before.

For Beto, who had become a witness to those abuses, it was terrible. On the other hand, he had to play a role he didn't like. He became the favorite executioner of his superiors.

He remembered the faces of those he once considered friends and were now mere strangers. "I'm sorry, Rafael." "I'm sorry, Antonio." "I'm sorry, so-and-so." "I'm sorry, employee number 7649." All phrases starting with "I'm sorry" ended with "you're fired." Those were the hardest words for him to say. But he had to. There was no option. Rebelling was improbable, and opposing his own company would have only given him the same outcome as the many who left before him.

For many, Beto was an honorary employee, a dinosaur waiting patiently for retirement. They weren't entirely wrong, but Beto was struggling to be patient.

He fought daily with the little recognition he received, with the new labor policies, with the profile of the new employees who didn't know how to listen or debate. He struggled with the conditions of his job, which were increasingly complicated and inhumane. This was not the same company he had entered so many years ago. It was not that majestic and perfect company where competition was intense but respectful, where salaries were enough for everyone, and where those with a family were valued and encouraged. Everything had changed.

Now Beto felt like a lab rat, condemned to press a button endlessly. The biggest challenge was enduring the tedium of inaction; he would have liked to innovate and try different things. Just a few years ago, he had presented a project to change certain aspects of the coordination he managed. It was denied. Too risky, too controversial, too different.

Another employee entered Beto's office. Despite the glass walls, Beto didn't notice him. He was absorbed in thoughts about numbers, payments, and years, thinking at the speed of light and with a heavy load of stress. The other person's voice alarmed him:

"Good morning, Mr. Beto," she said.

"Hello, hello, Gema, good day."

"I'm afraid it's not so good. We just received feedback on the last project. They want to see you in Mr. Ángel's office. You'll go on behalf of the team. That's what they decided."

Beto was unfazed.

"Perfect," he said with a feigned smile.

"It's in an hour. We sent you an email with the compiled information in case they ask you more questions."

"Thank you, Gema. Can I ask why you're so nervous?" he dared to ask.

Gema, surprisingly, took a chair and sat down. She dropped her head into her hands and sobbed. Beto was at the limit of confusion.

"It's just that all this is so stressful, you know, Mr. Beto? I thought it would be very different. But the deadlines always beat me, and the clients treat me badly, and then, the HR lady, I'm sure she has something against me because she really behaves horribly. This is definitely not the job of my dreams, and I feel exhausted and like I have no time now. I feel so stupid telling you all this. You wouldn't understand. I'm afraid of that meeting you're going to because I feel like my results weren't good. I know I don't stand out in the group, and we all fear that if they want to talk to you, it's because maybe it's bad news."

Beto remained silent. All he managed to do was pour a glass of water for Gema and hand it to her. He wanted to put his hands on her shoulders and tell her to calm down. He doesn't dare to touch her because he doesn't want his intentions to be misunderstood; he also can't tell her that everything is fine because clearly it's not.

"What did you study, Gema?"

"I have a degree in marketing; I also have several diplomas in social media management, advertising..."

"Ok," he interrupts her, "and do you have a family?"

"Well, my parents..."

"Do you still live with them?"

Gema doesn't answer immediately.

"I plan to move out in three months," she replies with embarrassment and anger.

"Very well. I have a daughter almost your age. She studied Biology. She wanted to enter the academic world, but well, she hasn't managed it. Now, she's in the pharmaceutical industry. And she also hates it. I can't understand you, Gema. Sadly, when I was your age, everything was very different. I'm not saying better, but different. I don't want to bore you with 'old people' stuff, but I'll give you some advice: don't condemn yourself to what they want from you."

Gema looks at him attentively. She's no longer crying. It seems it was a sentimental impulse. She nods her head and gets up from the seat.

"Thank you, Mr. Beto," she walks to the door and sighs before leaving.

She leaves, and he understands that he was of no help. Talking about his daughter? Referring to the "old"? Suddenly, Beto feels he has many thoughts that want to escape, but he doesn't know how to arrange them and let them out. He manages to open a program on his computer and takes care of writing during the time remaining before the meeting. He should be verifying expenses, but he feels too bewildered for that.

He arrives on time in the boardroom. In front of him, there are four more people. Only two are approximately his age. Beto isn't nervous. He senses this isn't about a dismissal or anything similar. After so many years, he can smell in the atmosphere what it's about.

"How's everything, Beto?" a woman asks.

"Tired, strange, confused."

One of the older men lets out a muffled laugh.

"Beto, colleague, always sincere. That's what we like about you."

"Thank you," Beto replies, "how did we do? What's it about?"

The same woman who started talking sighs and shows him a folder. Beto flips through it and knows perfectly well that this is the information he collected. Years ago, these sheets showed more seriousness and less color. Today, the tables, the graphs, everything needs dynamism and fresh colors.

"The numbers," Beto starts, "are very low."

"Indeed," says the woman.

"Translate this information for us," says another man.

"Right away," says Beto.

He picks up a marker and heads to a whiteboard that's tucked away in a corner of the room. Almost no one uses it anymore because everyone prefers to use the projectors.

In a flash, Beto explains the market circumstances that caused sales to drop; he also explains the prospects for the upcoming dates; he talks about trends and strategies. Agilely and vivaciously, he answers all the questions his superiors pose. They are satisfied with the explanations and even smile at certain jokes Beto makes.

"This has always been your favorite part of the job, hasn't it, Beto?" asks one of his colleagues, who is about the same age.

"Yes. I've always told them to hire an assistant to fill in the dynamic tables and do the tedious work. My thing is selling and standing up for my team and my results," he answers proudly.

"Aren't you tired yet?" asks the woman, who is younger.

"Not a bit."

"Thank you very much for everything, Beto. We'll send you an email with the minutes of the meeting and gather your team for new strategies. You shared valuable information with us today."

Beto says goodbye and leaves. As he closes the door, he knows that the people inside are wondering about his age. They want to know how much time they have left to employ him.

Everything seems to have gone well, but Beto is not sure about it. He learned that results do not always reflect permanence in the company. He remembers faces, especially of successful and triumphant people. Like him, they won awards and trophies in their professional life. However, the job market is so fickle that many were fired days later. Loyalty in companies is a myth. It does not serve to achieve stability. It's a survival game.

Beto knows that he has positioned himself as a valuable being within the company, but not for his charisma, his eloquence, his understanding of the market, and the numbers. It's because he has done what they asked, adhered to the guidelines, and helped them get what they need. In many cases, that meant firing his colleagues.

He has been loyal, but he does not trust that it is reciprocal.

Back in his office, he continues typing on his computer. He receives one email after another. He addresses them automatically, setting meeting times. Then he drinks another coffee and heads to his team. He is about twenty-five years older than all of them. He is a true relic, as they call him.

"Hello, everyone, I had a meeting today. It went badly. Does anyone know why?"

There is no relaxed face or voice that can answer. Then Beto understands that he is valuable because he has the necessary experience to make another group of individuals follow orders and achieve certain numbers. Without him, they couldn't. And Beto was lucky to have remained in his position and gained more experience. He was lucky not to have been disruptive or impatient. He was lucky that his fear always kept him within the margin expected by his company, and he was lucky that standing still meant staying there and being the only one out of thousands who became an expert leader. He never moved up from manager, although he longed for it. He never demanded less work despite being exploited. Congratulations, Beto. You were not the most excellent of your colleagues, but you were the most comfortable, and that is rewarded with retirement. But remember, Beto's case is one in a million.

In the meeting in front of so many young people, Beto realizes this. The advice he gave to Gema is totally the opposite of what he has done throughout his life.

But should we expect those who come after us to live life as we have lived it?

Beto has always been a number. Mr. Alberto Ramírez is just another number. He has always been conceived as a human with specific tasks. He should not do more or less. There is no place for that. His job is to achieve goals A and B. Nothing more.

More than half of his life has been given to the same company. He has spent more waking hours in his office than he has in his home. During his vacations, he was always available to his superiors, always answering important dates if he was sought after. He completely adapted to the system, so much so that he didn't even realize it. He has given his life, and now he just hopes to be paid correctly in return.

His fear in front of the display case is because he does not want to see himself aging. He does not want to accept that he is no longer the person who once won awards and was the best and most recognized in his company.

On his way home, he ponders his situation and his "luck." He asks himself whether it would have been better if he had been fired years ago so that he would have been forced to start a business and - possibly - find his vocation. He thinks about his own question to

Gema, "What did you study?" and realizes that his degree was never his greatest passion. He graduated in Accounting, but the truth is that he always wanted to be a pastry chef. Of course, his family disapproved of this outright. His father handed him a brochure of the career he wanted for him, and there was no more discussion or debate. Mr. Beto became a salesman and accountant.

At twenty-four, he got married. He had already acquired his first home. At twenty-six, he had his first child. At thirty, he thought about investing in a pastry shop. His company convinced him with bonuses and promotions, and his wife reminded him that they already had three children and that he couldn't take such a big risk. Yes, Beto's times were very different. However, fear was also an unpleasant ingredient within the professional field.

Behind you, there are thousands more who want your position; many of them can develop it in less time and for less money; many of them face greater dilemmas than yours and believe that working from sunrise to sunset is the solution. After all, most jobs are about executing. That is relatively "simple."

Worldwide, there is a trend for acquiring more technological innovations and robots that replace human strength. At first, the exemplification of this trend consisted of fast robots that operated levers on faster sliding belts that moved products within factories. Initially, robots were in the manufacturing sector.

Currently, this trend permeates customer service. There is an increasingly lower probability that a human will answer you when you try to dial a phone or send a message online. There are bots and robots intelligent enough to resolve doubts and solve problems or to exasperate you due to the lack of an ingenious human who understands you from the other side of the line.

There are countless bank employees who are losing their jobs because the remote service they provided to customers is no longer necessary. We are talking about thousands of people who have been replaced by ATMs, answering machines, and sophisticated algorithms.

Your ability will never surpass the automation of a machine; the machine will never surpass your humanity.

Where does the value of the employee lie? Evidently, if he was never hired for his unique and differentiating characteristics, he will not have permanence for such reasons. Remember that employees are generally just one more, another number, a simple payroll.

On the other hand, the pension system is in crisis worldwide. In countries where there are fewer young people, governments struggle to collect the contributions intended for retirement.

Without enough money, it is impossible to afford the lives and needs of the elderly. Retirees receive a very small percentage of their salary. It is not enough, especially due to the increase in their illnesses. The life of an elderly person is expensive.

An extreme case of this crisis is Japan, where vandalism and delinquency by the elderly have been reported with the aim of being admitted to prison. In this place, at least, they have guaranteed food and medicine. Outside, on the streets or in their homes, they do not have enough.

The pyramid of young people and the elderly is completely inverted in this Asian country. To make matters worse, their levels of work stress are extremely high. There is even a precise word in Japanese to designate death caused by overwork: karoshi.

To decide whether a person died due to their job, the determining factor is the hours of work. If it is proven that the deceased worked a hundred extra hours in the last month or eighty in the last two months (160 in two months), both the government and the company must pay compensation to the family.

The cases in Japan of karoshi are thousands; it is estimated that they equal the number of deaths from car accidents each year. People who suffer a karoshi collapse over their desks either from a heart attack or a stroke. Fatigue, stress, and demand are their killers.

Supposedly, this social phenomenon does not only happen in Japan. Heart attacks among young people may not be very frequent, but the origin of other atypical diseases is.

Above all, there is a worldwide trend in the increase of mental illnesses. The shadows of depression or anxiety pursue millions. At the end of the day, the question is reduced to what we need to be happy and balanced.

The Quality of Your Consumption

In the streets, in-store displays, in shops and department stores, on social media, in mundane conversations, and through television and movies, we are persuaded of one thing: genuinely happy people are millionaires.

We've been conditioned to believe they have no worries, that their lives are tremendously fun and spontaneous, and that nothing concerns them because they can solve everything with their plastic cards.

This vision of happiness began in the United States and has been perfectly crafted and reproduced to keep people distracted and constantly active. On September 11, 2001, one of the most cruel and shocking events in U.S. history occurred. Two business towers collapsed due to a terrorist attack on a plane, resulting in many deaths and injuries. The next day, then-President George W. Bush urged citizens to go out and shop to activate their economy to overcome the tragedy.

"Buy, work, acquire, and store?" Sure, they needed to support their country, but the fact that the president gave such instruction in such a delicate situation was strong evidence of the prevailing thought system in the United States, extended worldwide: you must consume, and your value is measured and based on your consumption.

During the Great Depression, an American merchant named Bernard London devised a system to force people to consume more. He did it intending to produce more money and liquidity and also to reactivate the money flow.

Today, his system is known as planned obsolescence. This means the products sold to us could last longer, but they are designed with a certain "expiry date." Moreover, there are other practices to make you get rid of your still-functional devices and objects to renew and stay trendy. It's called fashion and works by seasons, or it's called fashion and works by versions. Apple has used this model to achieve high sales. Their positioning campaigns are so successful that people buy their "iPhone" without reading about the operating systems or new features. They simply justify it with "I need it."

It's proven that after earning a certain amount monthly (in the U.S., $50,000), people's happiness doesn't increase. That is, a person earning $46,000 is as happy (or even more) than someone paid two million.

Happiness is not in possessions. It comes from within, your being. It's related to the people around you, the thoughts and feelings within you, your beliefs, and your experiences.

Happiness is achieved when we balance our needs and freedoms. Then, what we "want" naturally comes to us. We see obstacles less as fear and stress; they become opportunities. From them, we learn and grow stronger. Keeping our hearts strong is advice for true happiness.

How to achieve this sublime happiness in a world of 7.53 billion people? Can we raise our voices and demand better work conditions? How can we block reminders of the need to buy and consume?

Work, in theory, should meet our basic needs and provide stability and security. However, it has become a huge fear. Imagine a company controlled, managed, and executed by Chihuahua dogs. One dog makes copies, another serves coffee, and another prepares a meeting. There's a pack gossiping about another lone Chihuahua. On the upper floors, Chihuahuas fight, throw papers at each other, and some even bite.

Everyone is afraid. There's no guarantee you'll have the same job in two years. It depends not only on your superiors' decisions but also on your performance, home issues, and health. However, let's remind all these nervous and scared Chihuahuas: there are no certainties in life. Uncertainty in any aspect weakens everything. But have confidence that when we free ourselves from the tension of permanence, things flow.

In 2017, 54.8 percent of the population was urban. Despite the global problem of unemployment or poor working conditions, the reality of the countryside is very different from the city.

In the city, the supply of products doesn't completely depend on the seasons. Many fruits and vegetables are found in supermarkets year-round. In the countryside, people learn which foods are seasonal and use them accordingly.

City life involves increased expenses and a wider range of options. There are many activities, places, people, and much pollution. These elements wear down the health of city dwellers, even though they have health centers and medicines nearby.

As for work hours, the tasks in the countryside differ greatly from the city. For domestic matters in the city, many people can do it for you, or the government or private sector take care of infrastructure and street and service improvements.

In the countryside, brigades of residents improve their area. They face different challenges, especially in direct relation to nature, flora, and fauna.

In both environments, work is required and extends to other aspects of life. In both, there's the possibility of entrepreneurship, stepping out of the system, and deciding what you want for your life.

Does your job fulfill you? Does it satisfy you? Does it scare you?

THE LONG-LIVED HERO

Beto dreads seeing himself in that showcase of dusty trophies because what his reflection shows him is the sad countenance of a Chihuahua. He looks away in shame, pain, and fear. He knows that both he and his reflection await the moment to be called and dismissed or called and retired. The thought of having a noose around his neck for so long terrifies him. Sometimes, the knot has loosened, sometimes, it has been so tight that it forced him to do things he is not proud of.

For instance, he regrets not being there for his wife's third childbirth. He chose to stay for extra hours at work, trusting he would make it in time. On other occasions, he couldn't take care of his sick children or was so terrified of getting sick himself and losing his job or money that he faced worse consequences.

His job brings fears of different kinds: financial fears of not being able to provide, social fears of not standing out like his colleagues or maintaining friendships due to excessive work, and fear of the future due to the dire situation of retirement.

Beto, like most employees in the world, lives the collective anguish of losing his job or not having enough money. Beto, like most, works unpaid overtime, endures abuses and excesses, and ultimately gives all his capacity and innovation to a company that doesn't recognize him by his name and surname.

Months pass, and Beto continues in his office. Interestingly, he has become the counselor of younger employees. Ever since Gema dared to share her feelings with him that one time, Beto has listened in complicity to a dozen more. Now, he also fears for the health of his colleagues.

In the monthly meeting with a coach hired by the company to maintain the mental stability of its employees, Beto realizes his retirement is near. The coach's behavior has changed, steering the entire session towards Beto's future plans. "I'd like to tell you that I plan to travel a lot and enjoy time with my wife, but we won't have enough money," Beto confesses. "Why do you think that? You're one of the longest-serving employees." "Yes," interrupts Beto, "and the most reliable, the best executor, and, surely, you don't know this, but also the one who has received the most trophies and best sales. Yes, that's me. And? Do you think that ensures me anything? Ha! How old are you?" asks Beto, agitated. "I'm 34, Beto." "I'm 59. I know a bit more than you through my own experience. Tell me, do you like your job?" "Of course, I enjoy it immensely," lies the coach. "Perfect. Do me a favor and write down your personal email on a paper. I already know what I'll do after my retirement, and I'd like to tell you about it." The coach does as Beto asks, smiles worriedly, and lets him leave before the meeting ends. He can't imagine what Beto will do.

Months later, the general coordination throws a party to bid farewell to Mr. Beto, who becomes a legend for retiring after more than three decades of service. He isn't tired, rusty, or an old man in a wheelchair. He's an experienced adult man. He won the battle in the eyes of those applauding him as he receives his last recognition. Many shake his hand, pat his back, and congratulate him.

He leaves the office with very few things. As a precautious man, he started emptying his space months in advance. At home, his wife prepares his favorite meal, and his children arrive with bottles of wine and desserts. Mentally, Beto also includes his children in his retirement plan.

That same night, after the feast, laughter, and affection, Beto enters his study and sits at his computer. He writes a brief, concise letter to his former colleagues and his children: "To all of you, I know and value you. I have shared long hours of my life with you, knowing you subtly and precisely. I possibly know you in one of your worst facets: I've seen you victims of stress and anxiety. Thirty-seven years ago, when I joined the company at one of the lowest positions, I envisioned this day. From my home to school, I was sold the idea that if I worked hard for many years, I would become a retiree. I achieved what I set out to do, and I am a retiree, but an unhealthy and insecure one. I was told that my job would provide me with well-being and peace. They even said that my salary would suffice. It was a lie. Many times my wife and I had to work to pay rent, schools, and medical services. I am not against both of us working, but it was due to a cruel necessity, not for personal and professional development. Did I find peace in my job? Of course not. Month after month, I had to present numbers and translate statistics. I knew that if something went wrong, they would fire me or someone from my team. Possibly, those red numbers were just a scratch for the company, but for the employee, it can lead to suicide. Nor did I find well-being. I lost many years of my life working for a mission I still don't understand. My vision is not the company's vision, and for many years, I knew it was my mistake to stay in a place where I wasn't happy, but who would pay for our vacations? Who would feed us? Now I know that I lacked the courage to venture out. I should have sold myself and recognized my unique and invaluable value. I should have delved into understanding why I pressed the buttons I was instructed to press. I should have understood my passion. I see so many young colleagues affected with very high levels of anxiety and stress when their problems are not so enormous. For now, they only need to take care of themselves, and this is already too complicated for them. I'm not belittling them. What I mean is that if working conditions are so terrible for you now, how will you survive later? Don't buy other people's dreams, don't succumb to mechanical instructions, and don't give more than half of your life to nonsense. Strive so that your professional achievements bear your signature, your love, and your essence. Strive to spend more time with your children, partners, friends, and relatives. Have hobbies, skills, and external activities. Fall in love day by day with who you are. Only with mental peace will work be an extension of our well-being scheme. Only by convincing ourselves that nothing is permanent will we employ ourselves in finding the activity that completely fills us. I wish you peace, fulfillment, well-being, and clarity. Don't disregard the words of this 'old' employee who, after so long, was able to see the obvious. Sincerely, Beto." He hits the send button and sends his message to a hundred people. The following Monday, the text becomes a topic of conversation. It was a novelty until the employees demanded more numbers and more sales. There were layoffs and cuts. The cycle continued, and Beto's message got lost among messages and emails.

He didn't expect more. He trusted to impact at least one person. He wanted to settle a debt with himself and release the whirlwind of thoughts that had entangled him during his last months as an employee.

Not everyone is ready to hear something that forces them to move and activate. Are you ready?

THE INVASION

You open your eyes slowly and notice silhouettes at your bedroom door. They seem eager and kind; as every morning, they bring breakfast to your bed. They wait for you to stretch and yawn a bit. Then they approach, adjust your pillows for comfort and help you sit up. They unfold a table over your lap and place the plate. Breakfast is ready.

Your omelet, steaming and tasty, looks delicious, filled just the way you like. They never fail to serve you this way.

As you eat and enjoy the music they play for you, others fill the bathtub in the bathroom. When you step in, the water will be delightful; the temperature will be perfect. They add aromatic salts and ensure there's never a shortage of soap or shampoo.

They arrange the robe and towels so you can reach them effortlessly.

While you bathe, they clean your room, tidy the rest of the house, and prepare more coffee.

When you exit the bathroom, your clothes are selected and ironed for you. They think of everything.

There are a dozen Chihuahua dogs at your service. They strive to please and serve you. They are loyal and fear abandonment. They will do everything to ensure you don't leave them, and they do it so well you might not even notice them. They become invisible.

You're drinking coffee before leaving for work, and this pack brings you a newspaper written especially for you.

The headline reads "The News of Your Heart." Written in an eight-column format, it contains much information but exclusively about you. There are no hurricanes, stock market ups and downs, or government changes. In this newspaper, you'll find what worries you, what makes you jealous, what torments you, and the new mysteries approaching your life that rob you of sleep.

"Let's see," you murmur and start reading:

Alert: Mariela is taking longer to reply to your emails.

It has been reported that Mariela Cortés's response time to your messages has increased. The last one she replied to was the Friday before last, and her tone was one of boredom. She didn't seem enthusiastic or willing to go out, as you had proposed.

You met Mariela Cortés at a company party and approached her for a chat. That was your first encounter. You talked about the company, your professions, Peru, and the delicate political situation.

You exchanged phone numbers and have been texting each other for three months.

Attempts have been made to go out, but plans are always postponed for various reasons.

The recommendation of your personal and sentimental advisory board is to abandon any attempt at conversation, gossip, or invitation with Mariela Cortés.

You close the newspaper with some frustration. You see that a dozen dogs cleaning the kitchen, arranging your shoes, offering to refill your cup. You know they're right that you shouldn't talk to Mariela again. If she hasn't responded, it's because she's not interested. Yet, a part of you wants to keep talking to her, to try. Maybe she hasn't answered because she's too busy, perhaps with a lot of work.

You scratch your chin to hide your nervousness. You know these dogs detect this feeling and will try to dissuade and distract you if they recognize the anxiety and nerves.

You decline more coffee, say goodbye, and get into your car. There you're safe, you think, there you can remember and think more calmly. At home, you're a hostage. One treated very cordially, with all the care and services, but a hostage nonetheless.

Driving to work, you think about Mariela, not just about her and her person but about how hard it has been to find someone. This thought takes you back to when you presented an engagement ring.

You remember the butterflies in your stomach, the trembling. You planned every detail in advance so she would say yes.

After all, you both claimed to love each other deeply.

There was no way she would say no when you asked her to marry you.

So, you took her to that place for dinner, knelt, and took out the ring. You called her name with all the love in the world and smiled at her with tears in your eyes. Then you asked her, and she didn't immediately answer.

You kept smiling as she cried and seemed unable to speak due to crying. And you waited, but she didn't answer. Your legs trembled even more when you recognized that look of fear on her face. You knew she was going to refuse, that her tears were of anguish and pain. You anticipated the "no": the answer you never imagined.

Did it mean she was pretending to be happy? Didn't she want to be with you? Then why did she spend so much time with you? Why did she say she loved you?

She explains that it's about age that she doesn't feel ready. You sense they are excuses. You don't want to say it because you know it's a cliché, but you want to ask her...

"Is there someone else?" you blurt out the question.

She doesn't immediately respond, either. She doesn't want to hurt you, but her silence is more painful.

Once again, you know the answer without her saying it. You put the ring back in your pocket and leave. She tries to stop you, to say something, to make you listen, and you just want to save yourself the pain. Each of her words would be like a blow. You don't want to listen and, obviously, you leave. For you, her "no" is absolute. It's a no to the future, a no to us, a no to you and what you mean.

That experience left you feeling not good enough, that there's always someone else, that you won't be chosen or loved. People don't have the time or willingness for you because you believe they will never be ready.

That experience will define the next ones because it causes you fear and a lot of pain. You wouldn't want to live through it again, wouldn't want to be the recipient of that coarse look of pity and regret. No, you've decided, and the experience of love, marriage, and the union of two people is not for you.

You tell your friends you're better off alone; you lie to your parents, telling them you might find someone else, that now you're focused on your professional dimension. You repeat this story to yourself until you believe it. You think it's logical: you couldn't be a person in a family, it's not meant for you, you weren't "born" for this.

You believe so much in this version of yourself that you reproduce and reflect it in other areas of your life. Time and again, you convince yourself that you are the loner and that you can't change. It's not meant for you.

These types of disappointments have repeated themselves throughout your history; remember when you wanted to start your own company, and it didn't work? Do you recall when you expected your friend to do you a favor, but he said he didn't have the time? Remember when you asked for a raise and were met with a mocking smile?

While driving, you remember all these stories; you know that the newspaper your Chihuahua dogs give you every morning is a collection of threats and advice to keep you safe. You're convinced you write it yourself, that you give the dogs all the information to guide you properly. Do you know it, or do you want to convince yourself of it?

A part of you, one that fears this invasive pack of Chihuahua dogs, warns you that you're not alone in the car. Through the rearview mirror, you see an apparently harmless dog. It has its tongue out and looks nervously out the window. You also tense up and grip the steering wheel tighter. They never leave you; you're never alone. You take a deep breath and tell yourself what they try to convey with every look: they take care of you.

So, you turn to the dog and ask it to publish a special announcement in tomorrow's newspaper:

"I want on the front page a decree: from now on and for posterity, I am not interested in any romantic relationship. I am and want to be alone. I'm not interested in those things that once caught my attention so much. Do you understand?"

The dog doesn't bark or make any sound. For you, that's enough.

The scene would sound completely ridiculous and absurd to a third party. Of course, it is; it's false and unreal. However, it's a metaphor for everyday life. We let our fears feed us, pamper us, manage us, advise us, and tell us how to behave and what to believe in. Our fears seem to protect us from the wrong situations, from evil, and from pain. Wow, it even seems like our fears protect us from ourselves and our deepest desires.

Fears dress up in peaceful and passive ways. They seem harmless and look out for what's best for us.

If we combine this premise with what we've exposed in the chapters about the godfathers and godmothers of fear, it will be easy to detect the moments when our parents have instilled fears in us to protect us, where religion has advised us to hide in the cave of fear to obtain a great reward after severe hardships and lamentations; where culture has dictated that it's better to limit ourselves to feeling because it can hurt us, and then they teach us that certain archetypes or life models should be frightening.

However, the entrance of that pack of Chihuahuas into your car was your doing. The systems and subsystems permeate our lives, but they are not decisive or exclusive. We always have the door open to leave and reconfigure ourselves; we can always make the dogs leave. It's as simple as saying "shoo" or pretending to pick up a stone from the ground. However, you first need to gather courage and adopt.

The Absurd Party

I've often realized that we are what we believe we can be. This reality applies to both the positive and negative aspects of our lives. Consider the case of an alcoholic: only when they see themselves as a person with a problem will they understand that there's a solution. This is the exclusive path to change; our minds must already contain a certain possibility in order to achieve it. How can we achieve something that doesn't exist?

Think about the same person from the previous paragraph; by definition, an alcoholic is someone who consumes more alcohol than they can handle. It's estimated that a 70-kilogram individual can only drink 120 grams of pure alcohol. If a liter of beer equals 32 grams, we're talking about 3 liters, 750 milligrams of beer.

Other definitions suggest that an alcoholic is someone who, regardless of the amount, can't control their alcohol intake. Therefore, they drink too much and exhibit inappropriate behaviors. This primarily affects their health and social relationships but eventually infiltrates all aspects of their life.

Only when a person who needs to drink daily realizes that the bottle is controlling them, not the other way around, will they see this as a severe problem. Then, they might want to fix it, or they might postpone and justify not doing so. Either way, identifying the problem as a problem is the first step to the solution.

Justifications are usually stories we tell ourselves about ourselves. They are explanations we give to ourselves and then to others. With these, we aim to soften or disguise the problem and avoid the solution.

I once knew a couple with huge problems. It was a vicious circle where they both hurt each other. Talking with the husband, he confessed that he already knew she was like that - so jealous and angry - so there was no way to change it.

"Look, I already know how my wife is. Neither does she want to change, nor can I make her. The only solution is to endure her and for her to endure me," he said.

"But are you completely convinced that she can't change? Have you discussed it?"

"No, if we discuss it, it's sure to be worse and cause a big conflict... I have to understand her. After all, she has reasons to be so... so bitter. Her parents were very cruel to her, you know?"

I didn't want to continue the topic, so we talked about other matters. It wasn't the right time to tell him because he was defensive, but justifying ourselves with our past and life story isn't valid to explain why we can't change.

It's in our hands to understand how different circumstances have shaped and transformed us; it's in our hands to decide what we do with it, how we progress, and how we strive. Above all, it's in our hands to decide what we want to change into.

The problem often lies in not knowing what we need or what we will gain. Returning to the topic of the alcoholic, if they already know they have a problem, they also need to define what the result of applying the solution would be: would their social relationships improve, or would they lose the friends they usually go out drinking with? Could they create "easily," or would they suffer from not having that kind of "eureka" that alcohol offers them? Would they become a better father or brother, or would they enter a depressive and lonely situation?

These are answers that only the person with the problem can resolve. Perhaps for those without an addiction, the questions are very simple and boil down to being much better off without the drink, but once again, until the person with the conflict resolves it themselves, they won't know that the solution and instructions to improve their life are in their hands.

We incorrectly learn to satisfy ourselves with negative feelings. For example, many people vent their frustrations by creating fights with those they love the most. Others use guilt to alleviate their "pains." It's not fair that the person receiving the anger or guilt should have to endure it because the other doesn't know how to express themselves or recognize their emotions. It's not fair for the immature person to bear the consequences of their poorly thought-out actions.

If we learned to visualize what the result of our actions is or the person we can become, changing would be easier.

What prevents us from thinking of ourselves differently after the change? Primarily, we've been taught that it's impossible. The very godparents of fear have indoctrinated us to think that change is very complicated and that very few achieve it. On the other hand, change scares us because it represents the unknown and the imprecise.

As if it were a paradox, we've been taught that we deserve the whole world but have also been taught exclusively to build our perceptions and visions from fear.

Can you imagine if we could do it from another perspective?

Imagine we could step out of the absurd party where we so love to stay. It's a celebration where we rejoice in continuing in the job we hate, still traveling and mingling with those people who criticize us and contribute nothing, still not daring to be honest with ourselves, not yet confessing to those we love most that we love them with all our hearts.

It's the absurd party where we're not comfortable, but it's still a safe zone because at least we have the notion that we can partially control ourselves and what surrounds us. In the absurd party, we encounter our pathos and embrace it. We become an indissoluble mix of fear, comfort, and insecurity. We believe that we're better off there, that it's better to remain at the party and continue thinking of ourselves from our fears. If you were imagining this party, you'd know that there are thousands of Chihuahuas everywhere. They serve as much as they are served, tremble as much as they make others tremble, cuddle as much as they are cuddled.

Now imagine the door. The entrance is the same as the exit. No one is forced to enter this party. You can always leave. Do you see it at the back? It's wide open, and no one is leaving or saying goodbye. It's almost as if the threshold doesn't exist.

Do you really imagine we could leave this absurd party where we pretend to be happy? Of course, it's possible, and the solution is simple, but we often forget it. Would you dare to forget fear and conceptualize what surrounds you from love?

LOVE

How many times have we heard this word? It is used as a verb and deliberately. We say we love a certain TV show, a certain clothing brand, a person, or a specific activity. Social networks show us the number of couples and friends professing love for each other. However, have we stopped to ask ourselves what love is?

Love is another term that has been heavily influenced by culture. It has lost its universal characteristic and is sometimes used in different ways to benefit only a few. For example, in various religions, the concept of love is used to gain more loyalty and to promote fear. Therefore, I would like to start with the definition of love by clarifying that the antonym of love is not hate but fear.

Love drives, and fear paralyzes; love makes us happy, and fear makes us insecure and sad. Love is not just a nice feeling that makes us listen to music and see everything perfectly. Love is a quality and a capability: one loves and is loved. It's a decision and involves effort. It doesn't happen as we've been told: in the blink of an eye, overnight, with a sudden strike. No, love first demands knowledge of the object or subject to be loved. It's impossible to love what we don't know; it's impossible to love if we don't know how.

Discovering the other is magnificent; it means being able to step out of ourselves to understand those around us. Discovering that the other is a gift allows us to admire them and grow with their knowledge.

"Love is patient, love is kind. It does not envy, it does not boast, it is not proud. It does not dishonor others, it is not self-seeking, it is not easily angered, and it keeps no record of wrongs. Love does not delight in evil but rejoices with the truth. It always protects, always trusts, always hopes, always perseveres." Corinthians 13:4-7

Despite the beauty of this phrase, I want to clarify that the idea that love can endure everything has been misapplied to motivate people to endure violence and mistreatment. I invite you to ask yourself after reading this phrase: My own voluntary action of loving someone...

If it forgives, for what? If it believes, for what? If it waits, for what? If it endures, for what?

These doubts are extremely complicated because we haven't learned to love wisely. A fundamental premise is that love is perfect, and love, as a capacity, is unidirectional. Everyone decides who or what they love. It implies dedication. Although the loved one may come on their own, love does not grow without our will.

I like to exemplify the contradiction of love and fear with a scene from a brilliant movie called "Adaptation" written by screenwriter Charlie

Kaufman. In it, the main character and his brother are in a life-or-death moment and take the opportunity to thank each other for everything they've experienced and to confess certain frustrations.

The protagonist, who is anxious and fearful, tells his brother how it bothered him long ago when he saw girls mocking him, his brother. He explains that he witnessed from a distance how his brother approached one of them to confess his love and that when he turned his back and left, they laughed.

The protagonist says that it made him angry. Who were they to mock his brother's feelings? He even felt the laughter was directed at him.

But the brother tells him that he also heard the mocking but did nothing. He explains that it was because the love he felt was entirely his own, and nothing and no one could take it away from him.

"You are what you love, not what loves you."

Why exemplify fear and love with this scene? The first point is the sense of possession. Fear that doesn't respond to the survival instinct (which we've discussed in this book) is an external sensation that crouches us down, hides us, silences us, and subjugates us. Fear surrounds us and nests within us.

In contrast, love is born from us and therefore, when it's real, we control it. It's ours and it doesn't matter what battles we have to fight outside ourselves. If it's real and ours, it will be a gigantic engine. For example, Viktor Frankl narrates in his book "Man's

Search for Meaning" how he survived the concentration camp because the existence and memory of his wife motivated him. Even without knowing if she was still alive, possessing that love made him continue.

Love activates us, propels us, fills us, and encourages us. We have control over it because it's a personal decision; since it's individual, the first step towards real love is ourselves.

"Paradoxically, the ability to be alone is the condition for being able to love." Erich Fromm

Fear allies with ignorance to grow and take root. Love needs knowledge to become more real and profound. As we get to know the other and let the other know us - without pretenses, interests, or conditions - we are touching and learning to love. We stop hiding behind pretensions and absurdities; we are moving away from the empty and pathetic party to which our fears lead us.

Definitely, the brother in "Adaptation" conceptualizes his life from love and recognizes himself as a great source of it. He recognizes himself as a being capable of loving and being loved. He overcomes fear.

The protagonist, on the other hand, observes everything from the logic of fear. For him, life is a big complaint, a plot where he is a problem and where his abilities are not enough to make him happy. Fear takes over him, and he convinces himself that he cannot be loved or learn to love.

Fear confuses us.

Think of a man who sails his boat at sea. He goes out early to fish but has no luck. He decides to stay a few more hours; he needs fish to sell and make money. It's urgent. He remains vigilant, but nothing bites. He plans in his head where to move his boat to find fish.

He decides to do it and rearranges the bait and fishing rods. He sits and waits. Fatigue attacks him, and he falls asleep. When he wakes up, he finds himself in serious trouble. The sun has set, and the sea is very rough.

The man does his best to save himself. He doesn't even worry about the rods. It's urgent that he starts the engine and leaves. When he pulls the cable to activate the engine, he realizes there's no gasoline. Is there a leak? It's not the time to find out. He takes out some oars and positions them to use them. Behind him, the waves grow larger and larger. It starts to rain.

The man struggles but makes no progress. The sea plays with him at will. No matter how hard he tries, the power of the sea overwhelms him. He reaches the point where one wave lifts him, and another hits the belly of the small ship. It breaks in two, and the man is thrown into the air. He will probably die soon, he thinks. He believes everything is lost.

Surprisingly, he survives and makes it through the night. He finds a large piece of wood from his own boat and has managed to stay afloat. Around him is nothing but a calm and infinite ocean. He cries bitterly. He can't think of how to save himself.

Suddenly, a small boat appears a few hundred meters away. It's far, but he can see it. He can't make out how many people are traveling on it, but it's there. The man thinks of stretching and rising above the wood, but he's scared of hurting himself and, on top of that, of failing. Then he would be in a worse situation than he is now. He thinks about how he could draw the attention of the people on the boat, but since he doesn't see anyone, he decides not to do anything.

After a few brief minutes, he doesn't even see the boat anymore. He sighs and torments himself. "I should have done something," he mutters.

He keeps waiting. He hasn't tried to swim or look for land because he doesn't want to waste his energy. All he has left is to endure. Surprisingly, another boat appears. This one is larger, and there is movement on the deck. The man raises an arm. Nobody sees him; it seems something more interesting is happening on the other side because everyone is looking there. The man shakes one arm, then the other, then both at the same time.

"Look at me!" he shouts. "Please, here I am, help!"

Nothing. The people don't see him. The boat moves further away.

The man continues shouting; from so much effort, he gets tired and hoarse. He worries that another boat will come and he won't be able to hear it. He scolds himself:

"I shouldn't have stayed longer on the boat! I shouldn't have fallen asleep! I shouldn't have trusted that my boat was fine! I shouldn't have shouted or moved my arms! Now I'm lost, alone, hungry, and exhausted, and it's all my fault."

The man endures the sun and the changing tide, but he's afraid that some animal will eat him, that he'll completely dehydrate, and that his energy will run out.

After what seems like an eternity, another boat passes by, but this one is even bigger and more crowded. They are having a big party, and people are dancing and singing. Amid the tumult and excitement, no one hears the screams of the man who, from the water, is making his last attempts to be saved, but no one is interested.

Suddenly, one of the party attendees falls into the water. Some scream and their acquaintances also intend to jump in and save the person. Others stop them and look for ways to help the one who fell. They throw a large orange lifebuoy, and the person begins to swim towards it. With so much attention on the sea surface, someone else notices the shipwrecked man and shouts at him to swim towards the boat.

However, the man no longer has energy, is demotivated, and is terrified to move and fail. He doesn't want to suffer another disappointment. "I can't!" he shouts to those on the boat. They are slow to hear him, but they eventually do. "Yes, you can!" someone on the deck shouts. "Take the lifebuoy!" they implore. "But I can't... I can no longer move... If I let go of this board, I'll drown."

Despite not being heard, as the man is so weakened that he speaks more to himself than to others, another person shouts: "You must let go and swim!" "I'm afraid!" the man answers and cries. The party attendees observe him with concern and pity. They don't know what to do, waiting for a hero to jump in, but no one feels capable or wants to risk it. It's a regrettable scene. The person who had fallen into the sea is already back on the deck. "What's wrong with him?" someone asks. Another person shrugs. How could they imagine that the castaway's fear is greater than the ocean that threatens him?

WHEN YOU LET GO OF FEAR, YOU WILL NEVER BE THE SAME

Tony took a long time to understand that he was born without arms. He always felt complete, and his family made him feel loved and blessed from birth.

Due to a medication recommended to his mother for pregnancy symptoms like nausea and dizziness, Tony was born with malformations. He was born without arms, and in his country, Nicaragua, medicine was not as advanced as in the United States. That's why his family left everything to move there, trying to improve Tony's quality of life.

His parents didn't ponder long. It was an obvious decision. They would do anything within their capabilities to help their son.

Upon arriving in the United States, the attention was swift. After all, the drug Tony's mother took thalidomide, had affected many during that time. It didn't take long for the pharmaceutical industry to realize its mistake in allowing such a substance to be marketed. Naturally, they withdrew it from the market, but the terrible consequences were irreversible. There's no exact count of the affected, but it is known that about twelve thousand people around the world were born with malformations, and many others weren't even born.

Tony was one of the many cases in Latin America, as the drug produced in Germany was quickly exported to all continents. The United States was one of the countries that didn't approve it because it didn't meet all the requirements to be considered "reliable." This decision saved many lives.

Tony's parents were offered prosthetic arms and hands. They didn't reject the proposal, and their son began to use them. However, since birth, Tony had explored the world around him with his feet and legs. To him, the artificial arms were more like a burden or an obstacle. After several years of trying to use them properly and getting used to them, he decided to remove them. No one opposed it.

"Look, he has no arms!" people would shout in the street when they saw him. "Look, he has no arms," they whispered in his classroom or church. Tony Melendez was the armless boy, the incomplete, the pointed out. He got used to these shouts and whispers but never gave them much importance. After all, he was the owner of a joyful and dancing heart. His life was full of music, and he wouldn't allow a handful of comments to make him feel inferior.

He began to play with his father's guitar, an old handmade acoustic model from Ecuador. To Tony, as a child, it was an incredible toy. He plucked a string with his toe and heard a deep sound; another string, and now it was sharp. He learned to position his toes on the frets of the guitar and to produce fabulous notes and chords. He was thrilled by the sound.

He played a lot of music. He also learned to play the harmonica. Those who knew him admired his voice and told him so. Tony discovered that he was the armless boy and the one with the beautiful voice. Then, he decided to become a guitarist as well.

He practiced at least six hours daily, not even noticing the time because he enjoyed it immensely.

During his childhood, he discovered the church and Catholic religion, but it wasn't until his teenage years that he got closer and became part of the Sunday musical group. At first, he only sang in one mass; then, he spent all Sunday in the church with his group of friends and his guitar. There was something about lifting his voice to his creator that filled him so much and motivated him. Above all, he felt loved. He knew that, in front of God, he was complete.

This love he perceived was evident in his way of singing, composing, and performing. Gradually, his performances in the church became more and more famous until, one day, he was called for an event. He didn't know it was an audition to choose who would sing at a grand celebration, one that undoubtedly required his best notes and chords.

The news about the selection reached one of his acquaintances first. "Tony, I have to tell you something," this person said. "What is it?" "I was informed about something, something very exciting." Tony wondered what it could be, could it be true? "Is it about the test, about the audition? Do they want me to sing?" asked Tony, utterly surprised. "Yes, the invitation came from the organizers." "But, but me, really?" "Yes, Tony. I think you left them speechless with your great performance. You were amazing at the audition, now imagine at the event! Would you like to sing?" Tony breathed heavily, thrilled. He cried with happiness. "Of course! I'm ready, I'm happy! I'll sing. I'll play my guitar, of course."

This happened in the 1980s; it was the year 1987. Tony was a young man full of hope, life, and love. All of this was expressed in his way of singing and playing the guitar. It was the largest audience he had ever performed in front of. They showed him where to sit. It was a stage where only he and his guitar fit. In front of him was an aisle and after that, another much larger square stage. There, Pope John Paul II would be seated.

Tony sighed ecstatically when he arrived at the soundcheck. He indicated how he needed his guitar arranged. Then, he took advantage of the time he had before singing. He was nervous, but his joy was greater. He experienced an inspiring moment when he saw himself in a mirror before going out to sing. His smile was incomparable: pure and beautiful.

He was guided to his place and took a seat. He stretched out and approached the microphone. Everything was just as he needed it. Then he was introduced: "Now we have a special gift that we want to present. Our gift represents courage, the courage of self-motivation and family support. Our gift is music and the singer who says, "when I sing, I hear the

Lord." Holy Father, we are proud to present Tony Melendez."

The soft strumming of the strings, the precision in marking the notes... Tony moved the audience listening to him with the song titled "Never Be the Same." When he finished, applause fell on him like a tidal wave. Tony couldn't smile from the emotion. His entire body trembled with happiness for having been authentically an instrument of God through which a profound message was transmitted.

While the applause continued, Tony saw the white figure of the Pope, who approached. He maintained a demeanor full of peace and affection. His steps did not stop. He went to Tony. He jumped off the platform, crossed the aisle, and approached him. He stretched out his arms toward Tony while saying thank you. Tony also approached. The Pope took his face in his hands and kissed him. Tony returned the gesture and the smile. The Pope gave him another smile and returned to his place. He took his microphone and addressed Tony. "Tony," he exclaimed over the sound of applause and cheers, "you are a brave young man. A young man with much courage. You are giving hope to all of us. My wish for you is that you continue to give this hope to all people."

The applause continued, as did the shouts. Tony emitted a smile full of tenderness and courage. Never before had he realized what he was doing. Never before had he understood that he was not only performing his music for himself and his god, but that each letter, each second, was for others. His figure meant much more than the armless young guitarist. His voice sang beyond what the lyrics said.

Tony decided he had to do something for all those around him. He had previously attempted to become a priest but was stopped by the notion that he needed an index finger and a thumb to hold the host.

If he couldn't approach his fellow man through the status of a priest, he would achieve it through music. Thus, he began his ministries, which included programs, workshops, conferences, and concerts for young people and adults. Tony helps children with disabilities, like himself, to stop perceiving themselves only from "what they lack" and to identify more with the dignity that being children of God confers upon them.

His ministries also carry out projects in America, both North and Latin, that provide scholarships, funding, and community development.

Soon after, Tony met a wonderful woman to share the rest of his life with. Both share a love for music and God. For Tony, it was surprising to find someone like that because, for many years, he met many women who focused more on his appearance than the will of his soul. With his wife, everything was different. She detected from the beginning the wonder of Tony, his capacity, his sense of humor, and his vision.

Together, they adopted two children from Latin America and currently strive enormously to teach them to love and serve. The four form a beautiful family.

Tony Melendez is today a globally recognized artist; and an example of motivation, effort, hope, and love. From that day, the Holy Father entrusted him to be a vehicle of Christ's hope, Tony has not stopped nor will he stop.

The most uplifting thing about him is his ability to see miracles every day and everywhere. He himself explains that when he sees people at his concerts, he gets goosebumps, but the moment that brings him to tears is when everyone raises their hands. For Tony, the simple act of raising one's arms is a true miracle. To see a hand so perfect, so balanced, and so ready that is a miracle for him.

In his conferences and courses, Tony makes attendees see how complete and fortunate they are. He knows perfectly well that he, too, is a perfect and loved being; however, he will always be amazed by the perfection of the human body and the immense possibility of accepting ourselves and saying "yes."

Why did I want to tell you Tony Melendez's story? Because, in my opinion, it's the life story of a true hero who wasn't afraid of life itself but of eternal complaining and the tough question of 'Why me?' Tony never reduced himself to a comment or a completely certain fact. Obviously, he was someone who would have to work harder to master certain activities, but he achieved it. In fact, I played Frisbee with him a while ago. He catches the disc with his neck and throws it with his foot. He's much better than me, and not just because he tries harder, but because he trusts that he can do it.

From Tony, I learned something wonderful that I want to share with you. His house isn't infested with Chihuahuas, nor is his heart with anxiety, because he doesn't make room for fear. Tony focuses on what he does have rather than what he lacks.

Like Tony, there are many, many more cases of people who were born with some supposed limitation but who don't let this stop them. Their perception of fear is completely different because it's not unreal or illusory. They don't start from assumptions but from concrete facts: this is happening to me; how am I going to solve it?

For Tony, it would be very easy to complain day and night because he has no arms. If he only thought about that, he would never have been interested in the guitar and without his musical ability, he wouldn't have learned so many other things. Without his voice and his music, he would never have met the Pope and through him, his creator wouldn't have spoken to him so clearly.

Do you realize the wonderful adventure that life becomes when we dare to set aside fear? Do you notice the surprises, flavors, and colors offered to us at every moment? However, we refuse to see them because we haven't learned to detect miracles like

Tony does. For most of us, sadly, these are just ink marks on paper and not the words we need. For most, raising a hand is a boring and routine action, something simple and unimportant. It's so easy to do that we don't even value it.

When we find out that a person without arms played music for Pope John Paul II and that from that meeting, he was able to extract the motivation to help more and more people, we are moved. His message of hope is very clear: if he can, you can too. If he's not afraid, you shouldn't be either.

It's easy to say. It's simple to invite you not to be afraid without taking into consideration the different aspects of your life that lead you to stay still and without action. I know because I've also been in those moments, but I've worked and moved. What has motivated me the most is the great change I know I'm capable of making in others.

FOUR FEARFUL SEASONS

We like living in cycles, in fact, we celebrate them. Year after year, we celebrate certain days, and the New Year's celebration makes us nostalgic and optimistic. We enjoy the illusion that the bad or negative is gone and that we can relearn and reappreciate.

However, as long as we don't identify what holds us back and distracts us, we won't be able to change. I believe we live our lives more attached to seasons than we'd like to admit. Fear compels us to do this:

- The spring of sadomasochism

- The summer of false optimism

- The autumn of overwhelm

- The winter of misery

Let me start by explaining the spring: Flowers emerge from the ground and grow vigorously. They show off their colors as if it were a huge carnival. They strut in the breeze and offer the most delicious and productive pollen. In spring, flowers become true examples of nature's beauty. They are a visual spectacle.

In the spring of sadomasochism, we, too, show our colors and dance gracefully. However, we are completely limited to the space we occupy. Fear's godparents bury us so deeply that we can't leave this garden, and, what's worse, our presumptuous dance hurts and sinks us deeper.

Choosing the word 'sadomasochism' may be shocking, so I'd like to clarify. The Marquis de Sade, a notable French writer and public figure of the 18th century, was imprisoned for depravity. Yet, despite his crimes, what he did were the everyday activities of the French aristocracy; only he spoke about it openly, as he wrote extensively on the subject.

That's why I choose the word sadomasochism because we all repeat the actions of those around us, even though they harm and hurt us. If society tells us to follow a certain fashion, we do it. Sometimes, these fashions risk our physical and mental health, but we copy them. On other occasions, society limits us to a single color. And we comply, even though it's not our nature.

We hurt ourselves repeatedly, adjusting to rigid systems. The saddest part is that we do it knowing that we lose our mobility, freedom, and creative and expressive capacity. With so many gadgets and extra elements, we become flowers unable to share our pollen. Nothing more than a carnivalesque visual spectacle.

Generally, individuals experience the spring of sadomasochism in youth. We are wrapped up in belonging and being accepted. Such desires are so strong that they completely shape our way of thinking and acting.

Then comes the age of rebellion, of licentiousness. Our youth urges us to go beyond and break conformity, as not everyone follows this path of liberation, but we all know it, even if just by sight. Many are terrified to follow it, to leave the land that gently traps their roots and venture into the unknown. Many others do decide to renounce the systems; they may return. Either way, this is another stage experienced by men and women.

It's the summer of false optimism.

If we haven't completely unlearned the order stipulated by fear's godparents, we live in this stage because we believe we are outside the system. Finally, our pollen can be released, and so it is. We know what creativity, action, and freedom feel like. We can delve into many other issues that fear previously prevented us from exploring.

What we don't know is that our perceived fears will act in such a way that we won't see them, and suddenly, they'll return to us. Although we don't feel them above us nor see them as the figure of that trembling Chihuahua, we know they are lurking.

That's why our optimism is false. We know we have a specific time before the "age of grace" ends when society allows us to fail and dissent. Then we will return. We are made to believe.

Our roots will need the shelter of fear's godparents. We'll end up looking for the Chihuahuas in the closet, put on a leash, and give the other end to the dogs to take us back. We need society, family, and culture to survive. We tell ourselves this and don't lie. However, fear oppresses and reduces us to the extent that we completely forget what we were once able to create.

Almost all of us experience the autumn of overwhelm at some point in life. It's believing that everything is lost, that there's no way to undo the steps taken and reach the goals and dreams we once had. Past indifference, lack of action, and originality overwhelm us. Sadly, this overwhelm only plunges us deeper and deeper into chaotic feelings.

Consequently, we conclude our cycle with the winter of misery. Have our wrong decisions led us to this emotion? Has a lack of will and courage pushed us into misery?

The answer is ambivalent: yes and no. For many, misery is poverty, lack, and extreme need. Other people who seem to have everything also describe misery as abandonment and detachment.

We will all experience misery at some point, as well as overwhelm, false optimism, and sadomasochism. All of them are symptoms of the pressure of fear, but we can always change, as it's not about going back in our steps as we believe in the autumn of overwhelm. No, the same path that leads to the winter of misery is the same one that leads us to break so much ice and pain.

The winter of misery lives in us and freezes us. This is the complete submission to the invading pack. Winter makes us see everything through a prism of complaints and conformity. We definitely don't believe we're capable of moving forward, let alone reflecting or thinking. We fear that our own thoughts will point us out and diminish us. We are in the cold and unpleasant stillness and fear something even greater: dying without having transcended.

That is the misery and the paradox, knowing that we lead a life without meaning or precise milestones. We were here briefly and left without leaving a legacy.

Dear reader, please don't get overwhelmed, hurt yourself, lie to yourself, or feel miserable. Please, don't. All this can change instantly if you decide to change it. It's as easy as promising yourself that you won't try to fit into molds that don't suit you, that you will be honest with yourself because you are the best you have, that you will focus on what really matters, and that with all that and infusing love into your actions, you will transcend.

Do the following exercise that will open your eyes. You've probably already been advised to do it for healthy finances. Let's make a list of your assets, but I don't mean your properties or goods. This will be a list of your assets like your family, friends, job, and projects, to name a few.

Do you like horseback riding? That activity goes on this list as an asset to your happiness and health; if you are an enthusiast of art cinema or flamenco dancing, also note it.

How often do we forget those who love us, who push us, who support us, and who inspire us? Write down their names! Remember them and carry their teachings and enthusiasm with you. You'll notice that as you write, you'll also think of unpleasant people you have to deal with daily. These can be colleagues or family members. Don't focus on them. It's very difficult to get away from others it's almost impossible due to professional environments. However, you can shield yourself from their unconstructive comments or criticisms.

The purpose of the asset list is to find the elements that make us strive every day. It's about setting aside the pile of frustrating attitudes we've inherited. It's about truly blooming in spring, savoring the splendid winds of summer, enjoying the maturation of your fruits in autumn, and protecting yourself from the winter cold surrounded by your legacy and those you love most.

You've written your assets. Now, it's time for the liabilities. This list can be very, very long if we don't contrast it with the assets. Either way, in this section of the table, I just want you to write one liability. You must write what is stopping you so much from enjoying, relishing, and learning from your assets. What's limiting you?

The answer to this question is rooted in fear, but fear is not the complete answer. This is something deeper because it refers to a personal lack very identify by ourselves but that we dare not accept.

As we've already mentioned in previous chapters, some people are ready and willing to face their lacks because they've named them. Many others live in denial and don't know how to face what they lack.

It's almost like being outside the door of the room where you'll have the most important talk of your life, but there's no handle. You don't know how to enter.

You know what awaits you. In fact, you want that conversation to happen, but how to enter? The situation stresses and annoys you, the situation leads you through overwhelm and misery. You know that if you hadn't lied to yourself for so long or if you hadn't spent your creativity satisfying the requirements of the systems, you wouldn't be here.

Breathe, remember your assets. You'll be able to name your liability. And you'll be completely able to realize that the handle has been in your pocket all this time.

Rationalize Your Fears

Throughout these pages, we have delved into the origins and effects of fear. We now understand that there are two types of fear: one is real, and the other is perceived as real. One helps us to survive, the other makes us create fictions and live unhappily.

We have also exposed the systems and subsystems that legitimize perceived fear; we have discussed love as the reflective action that opposes fear. So, let's move to action. What do you need to ward off the pack, to stop behaving like a Chihuahua, to free yourself?

What are you willing to leave behind to overcome your fear?

Like a castaway at sea, you must use all your strength and energy to rationalize your fears. Understand where they come from, what feeds them, and why they continue to exist. Your fears have allies; have you identified them?

When you reflect and feel the absurdity with which you live daily, you will feel uncomfortable. Those houses of cards you have built around yourself will fall one by one. Everything that gave value to your life was formed from fear. Now that it's gone, what's left? Could you leave behind supposed friendships, beliefs, and a myriad of activities to stop being afraid?

I tell you in advance that it will not be easy, as you will be criticized and viewed as the boring person who leaves the party too soon because they have something to do. I'll let you know what you're going to be doing: working on your personal project, working on yourself, abandoning the latent murderer who has been chasing you for years.

To carry out this transition, answer the following questions. They are formulated so that you get closer to what you really want to be:

- What are you most afraid of?

- What do you love the most?

- What do you most want?

- Could you set aside your fears for what you love the most?

- Have you ever done it?

- When?

- What would you like to change?

Now, it's time to close the book and listen to yourself. Appreciate the opportunity to visualize the open door and reflect.

TERROR

If I give you a leash, would you put it on your faithful Chihuahua? Maybe you'll smile ironically and ask for thirty more leashes. But perhaps you'll smile with genuine enthusiasm and give me back a couple of used and worn collars. "Take these. Better ask me where my fears have taken me."

These are examples of the unexpected paths fear drags us down:

- "I lost the woman of my life because I was afraid she wouldn't like my appearance." A 33-year-old single man.
- "I couldn't witness my children growing up because I was wrapped up in being a 'model' mother and didn't pay attention to them." A mother of four children.
- "I lost my friends because I believed I was much better. I let my ego and fear of rejection lead my actions." A 27-year-old musician.
- "I don't talk to my daughter because I got scared and believed that her sexual preferences prevented her from being happy." The mother of a homosexual girl.

It's terrifying to realize that initial lack leads to more losses. Now imagine telling me where the absence of unreal or perceived fears has taken you.

- "I took a risk and spoke to who turned out to be the best partner, husband, and man for me." A woman was happy in her marriage.
- "I followed excellent advice and relaxed. Now I have the opportunity to continue living to see my grandchildren grow." A cancer survivor and grandmother.
- "I decided what I really needed, and now I'm one of the best ophthalmologists in my country." A young doctor whose father wanted him to study Commerce.
- "I stopped focusing on others and worked on what hurt me the most. Today, I want to help members of my community get closer to those they love the most." A religious minister.
- "I dared to take a huge leap and accept myself as I am. I won't allow anyone else to say if I'm pretty or not." A fire survivor.

I want you to write an epitaph for your fear. I want you to tell me that the pack no longer barks inside your head. I want you to taste the freedom of being yourself and knowing you are capable of loving and being loved. If excess fear leads to a lack of love, excess love leads to a lack of fear.

I want to conclude with a beautiful and ancient story. Many will find it familiar, but I hope that after this reading it can be better understood.

When Jesus died and then resurrected on the third day, the apostles had to hide for a while because they were sought after due to their closeness with

Jesus. They were frightened, full of terror and anxiety. Would they be able to fulfill the mission of evangelizing and conveying his message? How would they deal with being persecuted?

Their task meant a possible painful death. But desertion of their duty was a greater penalty: completely betraying Jesus's love.

We all know the outcome of their discernment. After Jesus granted them extraordinary powers and faculties, after he blessed them with a tongue of fire to endow them with wisdom and knowledge, the apostles dispersed throughout the world and transmitted the good news: Jesus had resurrected, and he was indeed the Son of God. Their message to humanity was, is, and will continue to be that we love one another.

That task is for all the sons and daughters of God. We all need to take risks, but with complete hope and confidence that we are protected by love. I hope your season in your own darkness ends and you come out of lethargy. Remember that this stage is necessary to decide bravely and conclude the season of our fears.

When we take the leap, we'll read books that start very differently, and you'll never identify with the first chapter of this book ever again.

Once again, you get up and feel rested. You love those nights when you sleep so well that it feels like twice the hours you actually slept. You feel like you lay down on the mattress, closed your eyes, and went to a spa party. It's wonderful.

You sit up and stretch. What will you do today? Will you enjoy your family, go out with friends, immerse yourself in your favorite activity, or be grateful for your satisfying job?

You look in the mirror near your bed and know that it really doesn't matter what activity you're going to do. You are happy and full of enthusiasm. From the mirror, smile back a healthy, fulfilled, and blessed person. In the mirror is the best smile in the world because it doesn't have fear but infinite love.

From outside your house, you hear a symphony of barks. You look out the window and see your Golden Retriever barking at the neighbor's dog. You whistle and call her by her name:

- *"Terror, stop, calm down!" Your pet gives you a candid and gentle look. She seems to smile. You go downstairs and take the leash. It's time for a walk.*

www.ingramcontent.com/pod-product-compliance
Lightning Source LLC
Chambersburg PA
CBHW071355120626

46546CB00002B/706